BAPTISM OF EXCITEMENT

A Memoir of War & Peace

BAPTISM OF EXCITEMENT

A Memoir of War & Peace

PHILIP MIDDLETON DAVIES

PHILIP MIDDLETON DAVIES
Baptism of Excitement – A Memoir of War & Peace

Published in partnership with Riverside Publishing Solutions

ISBN-13: 978-1-913012-57-1

Printed and bound in the United Kingdom

In memory of my wife, Mona (1928–2020) *and our elder daughter, Jackie* (1958–2020).
To our daughter, Jane and to our grandchildren, Jessica, Hugo and Oliver.

Contents

Introduction

This is a memoir of a man who, at the impressionable age of eight years old, lived in London at the start of World War II.

He endured the terrors of the Blitz over London 1940–41, and the subsequent horrors of war in the United Kingdom until 1945. He describes his feelings throughout as those of fear, of togetherness, and of a weakening of class deference.

The memoir goes on to tell of the Author's future, starting with National Service. With the throw of dice this leads him into a soldier's life. A voyage from Liverpool to Korea calling at Ceylon, Hong Kong, and Japan. What an adventure for a 20-year-old youngster starting in the world of work. An experience of excitement, constant moving, and troubleshooting too. A small cog in a huge army machine of 150,000 plus, the Author had to cope with many frustrations – not least degrading pay and conditions of service for all ranks; also frequent changes of plan at the highest level without any apparent regard for the families of those serving.

The reader will note that the Author only served in five of the military operations listed in the Epilogue. Nevertheless, the level of activity was brisk. What of the future?

What a start though. The Author lost his virginity aboard a ship halfway around the world to an enchanting lady just a touch older than his 20 years!

1

War Time 1939–1945

This tale of thick and thin really begins from being sent aged 7 to boarding school in 1939 on the eve of World War II. The school was in the leafy lanes of Ascot. It was called Earleywood, and has long since been closed. I certainly was not the youngest entry; I suspect we were hostage to fortune with parents anxious to get us out of London and away from the Blitz whilst resisting the possibility of evacuation.

I hated Prep school. I was bullied by older boys and beaten monthly if not weekly by the Headmaster Edward Aldrich Blake.

By 1939 all eligible school staff had or were about to be enlisted in the Armed Forces. As a result, we were taught mainly by elderly women. Amongst compulsory subjects were ancient Greek and Latin; the domain of an unforgettable defrocked priest who spent most of his time at The Berysteede Hotel en route to Ascot racecourse.

To lighten the tedious and seemingly useless burden of classics and algebra I chose to take piano lessons as an extra. What a mistake! On each wrong note that I hit my hair was mercilessly pulled. To this day I deeply regret my failure to stick with the piano. I do however still have a full head of hair! On a happier side, school sports were a huge relief to the challenging conditions indoors. Our main local school sports competitors were from prep schools such as Ludgrove, Sunningdale, and Woodcote House. I enjoyed rugby and cricket. I recall a key cricket match that we had to win. We were fielding and my position was deep by the boundary at 'long leg'. Normally a quiet spot but suddenly a huge hit by the batsman, high in the air towards 'long leg'. The sun was shining, and I had to catch the ball. My team were looking towards me and there was a hush around the ground! I spotted the ball high in the sky; it began its slow descent; I picked out the red colour looming larger like a red setting sun – how could I miss – I embraced the sun and caught the ball!

One might think that to a 7 to 12-year-old boy (1939–45) the conduct of the War was of passing interest. Not so, it was of great concern and brought some relief to our own internment. A good supply of newspapers was provided, and I remember especially being grabbed and occasionally excited by the headlines of The Times spread out on a reading frame. TOBRUK RELIEVED!

Continuing studies of ancient tongues and equations did not seem relevant to us boys at the time. However, there were to be diversions. Firstly, the Luftwaffe in aircraft either damaged or lost by poor navigation, would jettison bombs in our area. This precipitated huge excitement, often a scramble to be down ladders from dormitory to shelter, in the dark and with much shouting and laughter.

Another light-hearted diversion was the acquisition by the school of a cow. The idea of course being to ameliorate the desperate shortage of milk. What a playground! Two udders each and the fight was on!

My parents had separated in the 1930s; my mother, elder brother, David, and I lived in Primrose Hill near Lords cricket ground. My brother, 18 months older than me, led the way to scaling the walls at Lords as we found our way to the boundary grass to watch a day's cricket starring Wally Hammond, Len Hutton, and Bill Edrich amongst others. They batted in style as we sat with our lunch of packets of Smith's crisps at two pence (old money) a bag including a vital blue wrapping of salt. This was, of course, a school holiday activity. We both had scoring books, pencils, and rubbers, etc.

From time to time, we compared our records of play by the great men in the field. If you had missed a dot on the score card for a ball bowled then your reputation as a competent scorer suffered.

If not cricket, my favourite occupations in London were bicycling and trips to Regents Park Zoo to watch the penguins being fed fish by the keepers. During country holidays my brother and I fished, enjoyed cycling, and picking wild berries and mushrooms.

The fortitude of Londoners during the Blitz by German aircraft is legendary. The worse the bombing got, the stiffer became the back! Hitherto class division in England was rife. It broke down in an air of good humour and help between all.

The bombed out, the wounded, the helpless found comfort in shared plight. The will to win was never blighted. Fortified by visits to the East End by HM the King and Winston Churchill. There was of course immense freedom of movement in London by bicycle which my brother and I used to the full. In self- navigation of the streets of London we were years ahead of Satnav!

Air raid sirens were almost continuous. By day this was not a problem as you dumped your bike and ran for the nearest shelter. By night for us there were two options. First, a bed space in the porter's basement flat. Much more appealing was a short walk in the 'black out' to Regent's Park tube station. There down below, in a very dim and creepy light, were rows of wooden bunkbeds for the elderly or very young. The Women's Voluntary Service (WVS), the Red Cross, and many other helpers were there to provide comfort, hot soup, and endless tin mugs of tea.

When the 'All Clear' sounded everyone exited as fast as possible to get away from the stench of bodies young and old and of course to find out if your house was still standing.

Soon after the Blitz the family moved to West Sussex between West Chiltington and Storrington. What happy memories of roaming the countryside, picking blackberries and mushrooms in the autumn. Highlights for my brother and I were riding for several miles on our bicycles to fish on the bridge over the River Arun in Pulborough. The fact that neither my brother nor I could see over the bridge wall resulted in a slightly dampened level of excitement!

The war was of course never far away and in 1940–41 the Battle of Britain and the struggle for air supremacy was taking place almost over our heads. We watched in brilliant sunlight as young air crew from airfields all over England took on wave after wave of German bombers with fighter escorts.

Dad's Army really did exist almost as portrayed on television today. There were many members in the surrounding villages. They were initially equipped with wooden rifles and pitch forks. A wonderful group of men too old for active service but terrifying to German air crew bailing out of their aircraft often into local fields.

During five years of war for us youngsters there was excitement and not a few privations. One fresh egg a week or perhaps dried egg or even an egg kept safe in a bucket floating in some magic liquid! One pot of jam a month. Depending on your relationship with your butcher one glimpsed meat from time to time. Fruit, locally grown apart, was not available. I recall seeing and eating my first banana in 1945.

And so, during the next three years the war of attrition in Europe drew to a close; a result of heroism, self-sacrifice, military and civilian robustness and not least the help of our Allies. Despite hardship, shared by all, high morale, kindness, and generosity were boundless. In particular, the role played by women in the war should never be forgotten. Military service, working in munitions factories, cypher duties, ferrying aircraft, etc.

To a young man now 12 years old there are memories never to be forgotten and lessons to remember.

2
School

In 1946 off to school at Charterhouse aged 13, I joined my brother David in a schoolhouse called Robinites. What a change from the previous institution. The school atmosphere was outwardly relaxed, and I was not beaten once! School monitors did in those days have the authority to beat miscreants.

Academic work was a joy. Very professional. One explored English literature and language. French and German language were favourites of mine. Much attention was given to rhythm in the Music School and to the Arts, painting, and drama.

There was a thriving Combined Cadet Force (CCF). I joined and enjoyed the army side of CCF but was regrettably sacked as a bugler. Totally incompetent! The Church is quite beautiful and was much used. Three attendances on a Sunday; early Communion, Morning Prayer and Evensong!

The opportunities for sport were unbelievable not least cricket which at 1st XI level was played on one of the most beautiful grounds in England. In my time the star was Peter May who went on to Captain England. At school he was also Captain of soccer, hockey, and fives. John May, his brother wasn't bad either and I think made the first cricket XI at 15 years old. For my part I think I just made the 3rd XI for cricket, played soccer, fives, squash and racquets. A wonderful, positive, and happy experience. Sadly, I didn't last the full course because of funding. My mother had bravely coped with seeing us both through the war and school. My brother went straight from Charterhouse into National Service. It came as a blow to me to leave early just as school horizons were opening in study, sport, and responsibility. Never mind, I had to bite the bullet and find something to do before National Service.

Now 17 verging on 18 what to do. Everyone our age group knew they were earmarked for 2 years National Service – but when – it was the luck of the draw? My grandmother who lived in Ealing and survived much local bombing offered me a bed as I had to secure a job before National Service. In due course I was offered a job at Smee's Advertising Agency in Duke Street by Selfridges. It was a pretty humble and lowly paid job, but it kept me out of trouble for nearly a year before my National Service call up papers arrived.

3

National Service

On 4th January 1950 I reported, a touch scared, at Budbrooke Barracks, Warwickshire.

I was enlisted as a Private soldier in The Sherwood Foresters. I might have been a guardsman, a gunner, a trooper, or a sapper, but here I was, an infantryman!

On that memorable day, there were about 40 of us – all in the same boat – anxious, and many missing home already! There were about 20 of us in the tin-roofed barrack room, the centre piece being a black pot-bellied stove fed on coal.

As night-time loomed, I unpacked my suitcase and put my pyjamas on a straw- filled pillow on top of a straw-filled mattress! It was not long before I noted everyone getting into bed in their vest and pants. Did I dare to put on my pyjamas? No! It took me two nights to summon up courage. By then we were all mates, and nobody gave a stuff.

Day 2. Uniforms were issued and the practise of marching everywhere and saluting everything began. That very afternoon we were assembled in line outside a Medical hut. Word soon spread – we were there for injections. As we stood outside on that cold January afternoon, I can recall vividly new recruits like myself keeling over at the thought of the needle! I have to say fresh needles seemed to be in short supply! I have an idea that we were given a cocktail of an injection. This may be wrong – perhaps some sort of immunisation.

In any event, an early experience of the military jab(s) which pursued me throughout my army career.

We became used to a routine of drill and more drill, physical training, and more physical training, firing on the ranges and more. To be fair, I think the system of constant intakes of recruits was testing the system. What to do at Training Depot level? White paint was the answer! For years there cannot have been a kerb in any barracks in Warwickshire that had not been painted glistening white by the future defenders of the Kingdom.

It was not too long before I found myself on the first rung of a long ladder. Promoted to Lance Corporal! The height of responsibility was probably ironing the battle dress trousers of the squad Sergeant – with brown paper, of course! Some weeks later I was summoned to see the Commanding Officer and after a short interview was told to appear at a War Office Selection Board (WOSB) at Westbury in Wiltshire.

Our particular WOSB was in the Summer with a group of about 30 from all units in the Army. The Selection Board was meticulously conducted; each squad of 10 was supervised by a Lieutenant Colonel. A Major General was in charge, with a Brigadier as deputy! We had no names, just a bib with a large number back and front.

There were written tests, IQ tests, public speaking tests, map reading tests and above all, an obstacle course designed to test all aspects of our ability to lead. To get over an imaginary river with your team with ropes, planks, ladders all too short was the ultimate test! I was lucky enough to pass and after some weeks found myself en route for Eaton Hall Officer Cadet School (OCS) near Chester.

The course was 16 weeks of intensive infantry training the majority of which was conducted within the Grosvenor Estate and the magnificent residence. Cadets were organised into Companies commanded by Infantry Majors with operational experience.

The wonderful NCO instructors were mainly from the Guards Brigade headed at the time by the redoubtable Regimental Sergeant Major Britain.

It was in May 1950 that my mother married again. My new stepfather was Lt Col Charles Allen, MC. Exactly a year on, in May 1951, my half-sister, Caroline was born. I recall making my first visit home to see my new sister. Travelling by train from Cheshire to Suffolk in uniform was a long and tedious trip. After many hours I arrived at the cottage in Polstead, Stoke-by-Nayland, Suffolk. I walked through the garden to the front door where I took off my military beret to greet my mother. The door opens, an apparition appears all in white and starched stiff as cardboard. It looks me up and down and says in an equally starched voice “you don’t part your hair very nicely, do you?”! That was ‘her ladyship’s’ nanny. I did not remain dumbstruck for long!

4

Sandhurst

I have come to believe that one's path in life is almost chosen for you. There is a moment, an influence, or an incident which provides direction. For me it was the influence of my experience as a cadet at Eaton Hall that directed me to seek a regular military career. I should say at this juncture that in the year 1950 the Korean War erupted. Many cadets, shortly to be commissioned into infantry regiments were destined to join the Commonwealth Division in Korea. The realism and excitement of the 16-week courses at OCS thus gathered much pace and deadly seriousness.

So, before my course was completed, I had applied for a regular commission. In due course I found myself at Westbury again. This time in front of a Regular Commission Board (RCB). Happily, I passed the tests, very similar to WOSB. In 1951 I was an Officer Cadet again; this time in Old College, Dettingen Company at the Royal Military Academy Sandhurst (RMAS).

The course at RMAS at the time was run over two years, though now, I believe it is 44 weeks. On arrival as a new Officer Cadet, one enters Old College in some trepidation and make your way along flag stoned corridors and solid stone stairs to reach your room. There at a touch the tenseness vanishes. "I am Jack, your Servant, Sir." This comes as a considerable shock to real life but is so welcoming and timely! Sadly, but not surprisingly, the custom of Servants at RMAS stopped long ago. Nonetheless, Jack showed me around, explained the tough regime ahead and undertook to help out in any way permissible.

RMAS was a pretty balanced mixture of things military and further education in history, the sciences and the arts. It needs emphasising that Term One was pretty brutal. One was chased from pillar to post at much speed; at assorted times of the day. The grinding and seemingly never-ending drill on the square took place under supervision of NCOs of the Brigade of Guards. At first these wonderful, experienced soldiers were terrifying, but all had hearts of gold. It was primarily their job to test us to near breaking point to see if we had the stuffing for what lay ahead.

The most senior post in the RMAS Guards hierarchy was the Regimental Sergeant Major (RSM). At our time, the incumbent was RSM Jack Lord. A veteran of Arnhem, he was hugely respected by all the cadets and of course, by all his subordinates. As fierce as any man could be on the parade ground, yet not without a twinkle of humour. "Mister Davies, Sir, you are utterly useless to me, you are out of step, Sir." I was 6′4″ thus usually right marker. A sign of twinkling respect on both sides of the fence that pervaded Sandhurst. In retrospect we all loved Jack Lord.

There were of course many moments of fun. I recall a plot to flour bomb the nearby Women's Royal Army Corps (WRAC) cadet training college. Four of us went by day to the college and explained that our four sisters would like to know more as they were considering military careers. This approach was swallowed hook, line, and sinker! We were duly shown around the barracks including cadet accommodation, with great courtesy.

Some days later, armed only with flour bombs in paper bags, we launched our attack in the dark. It was over in seconds. Flour bags burst in puffs in the girl cadets' rooms amidst shrieks and laughter. We withdrew! The entire Academy at Sandhurst was paraded some days later to uncover the culprits of this dastardly act. The curtain was eventually drawn over a wall of silence.

It was towards the end of year one that potential regular officers had to declare their preferred Regiment. This usually caused initial or renewed activity between candidate and prospective choice of Regiment. I had no direct family association except perhaps that of my great-grandfather. He had won a contract to supply the Army in the Great War with jam. 'Ticklers Plum & Apple Jam' permeated the trenches from 1914. It was apparently so disliked by the soldiers that tins of the stuff were fired from mortars against the Bosche! In due course he produced the better known 'Nell Gwynne Marmalade'.

It so happened that my mother knew a very distinguished soldier, Brigadier Norman Crockatt who had fought with his Regiment, The Royal Scots in the Great War and was on Intelligence duties in World War II. Contact was made between me and Mrs Rose Crockatt. An interview was to follow with the Brigadier at their house in Virginia Water. I had been warned a game of tennis might be played. I duly arrived one afternoon with stuff for tennis in a bag. "Up you go and change, young man – I'll send a gin up" said Brigadier Norman. Down to the tennis court – "have another gin, young man" said the Brigadier "the others are just finishing off". And so, it was time for tea on the lawn. Tea came and went, and the Brigadier said, "We normally have a Pimm's, Philip before we finish off the tennis". At this point it hit me that I was being tested. Could I hold another drink down? An evening whisky followed. The climax to a long afternoon and interview was when Rose Crockatt said to me "your family are coming over for supper – you will stay, won't you?". I returned to Sandhurst with much care. Later I was to hear that I was acceptable for The Royal Scots provided I completed the course at RMAS in the top third.

It was at Sandhurst that Charles Tarver taught me how to cast a fly on the large lake in the grounds. The lake was regularly stocked with rainbow trout, and some brownies too. A couple of elderly rowing boats were available. From the lake we progressed to the Wish Stream – a permanent outlet from the lake and in the memory of every cadet as it formed part of a challenging assault course. A touch more casting skill was required on the Wish Stream. A skill taken on board by me and passed on years later to our two grandsons on Wiltshire visits.

What an experience at RMAS! Two years of leadership skills taught and supervised by an impeccable team of soldiers and civilians. The climax of course was the Passing Out Parade taken very often by a member of the Royal Family. It was my good fortune that King Hussein of Jordan was on parade as a senior cadet Passing Out. He was in Old College Blenheim Company. "Mister King Hussein, Sir" shouted RSM Lord "stop fidgeting in the ranks, Sir"! The parade finishes. The Adjutant mounts the steps of Old College on his grey charger. Senior cadets follow. The band plays. A final disturbance – a huge American car arrives on the Square, HM King Hussein leaps in and arrives for tea at The Dorchester!

5

A Long Journey

I suppose the next phase in a fast sequence of adjusting to a future in the military might be described as 'settling in'.

I was commissioned into The Royal Scots (The Royal Regiment) from RMA Sandhurst on 6th February 1953. Thereafter, one had to attend a very active young officer's course at the School of Infantry, Warminster. This was hotly followed by a Small Arms course at Hythe in Kent. Next problem was our regimental tailor, William Anderson & Sons was in George Street, Edinburgh! Much travel and several fittings were required for an assortment of kit. Of course, in those days you were not expected to pay your tailor direct. A charming way of doing business over the years – an expression of total trust sadly lacking today.

It was not long before I received a Notice and Travel Warrant to report to the Depot of The Royal Scots at Edinburgh. On my arrival I was courteously shown to my room where, looking slightly bemused, was a young man wearing glasses sitting on one of the two beds. It was John Knott of 10th Gurkhas and later to become Secretary of State for Defence! The 10th Gurkhas was a sister Regiment of the Royal Scots. We trained their Pipers who wore the regimental Hunting Stewart tartan. I was later lucky enough to serve alongside 10GR in Malaya and Cyprus during the 1974 troubles.

And so, the big day came! I was to join the 1st Battalion of The Royal Scots in Korea.

My instructions were pretty brisk: "Report to "Movements" Liverpool Docks to embark with 30 Jocks on Her Majesty's Troopship (HMT) Empire Fowey bound for Hong Kong".

I am bound to say my 30 Jocks were a pretty grim and tough-looking lot. For one reason or another they had "missed" the move with the 1st Battalion. At my first pay parade which, in those day involved extraordinary amounts of saluting and stamping of feet, Private McCabe steadfastly refused to take his pay, "I'm no taken it, Sir". I gave him no quarter and he marched away penniless. I suppose it was my first little test. Later, Bunty McCabe and I became good comrades. Fat and idle, but with a heart of oak!

Conditions of travel for junior soldiers on troopships in the 1950s were bad. Always on lower decks, without much air, with no views, and sleeping in hammocks. I make the point now because life onboard a P&O Troopship for a young officer was enviable. It was important, therefore, to visit daily the soldiers on lower decks and do what you could for them. It was vital that fitness for all ranks was maintained throughout the voyage. A day's routine aboard the troopship would be on the lines of:-

AM	BREAKFAST
	DAILY INSPECTION OF FEET AND LIVING QUARTERS
	WEAPON TRAINING
	VIGOROUS EXERCISE
	LECTURES
	MORE EXERCISE
PM	LUNCH
	DECK GAMES ACTIVITIES
	WEAPON FIRING OVER STERN OF SHIP
	LECTURES ON TACTICS, ETC

By 5pm soldiers were ready for tea. It might be thought strange, but in the infantry, feet are the engines which have to be cleaned and maintained.

There were all sorts aboard the Empire Fowey. No one unit, but a mixture of folk, senior, and young, women, and children, military and civilian, all travelling to re-join units or to reintegrate as families posted overseas.

Aged 20, on my first voyage, I was seduced firstly by the lifestyle and secondly, by an attractive lady who was either bored or naughty – perhaps both! With much aplomb she introduced me to her husband on arrival in Singapore! I get a head of myself.

Ceylon (Sri Lanka) was not listed as a stop-over, but the ship appeared to need some repair. I am reminded of a fairly common RAF practice to require a sudden maintenance stop-over to pick up a load of choice sea food for the oncoming Guest Night. We did not dally long in Ceylon but long enough for a magnificent curry and a bed for the night in the luxurious Galle Face Hotel.Colombo is well known for its rubies, but you need expertise, or you might be buying glass, Beware!

The next scheduled port of call was Hong Kong. This was a stepping-stone for me and my group of 30 soldiers. We were to undergo battle training for Korea. I remember disembarking from the Empire Fowey straight into the Peninsular Hotel.

Reality began the next day with a long, hot drive to a camp in the New Territories. The training would be conducted by the Welch Regiment, who had just finished a tour in Korea. We were rightly put through the wringer by the Welch. No doubt turned up a touch after they discovered the Jocks had sprayed green the Regimental Mascot.

I recall one night well. It was my 21st birthday and I was spending the night knee deep in monsoon rain in a trench, "Happy Birthday,

Philip" said the Commanding Officer, Lieutenant Colonel Bun Cowie while on his rounds.

And so, we went on by aircraft bound for Korea. Yet more difficulties, possibly due to the tense political/military situation at the time. In hindsight, a truce was in sight that remains extant to this day. We landed in Japan! I awaited instructions for onward movement to Korea. These were not forthcoming, and we were sent off for more battle training American style!

The penultimate stage of our long journey from Liverpool was by sea to Pusan, the principal military port in South Korea. A shaky truce had by now been declared through the United Nations; that did not preclude the most astonishing welcome we received from the US Army at Pusan dockside led by an all-black army band playing jazz music and wearing glistening silver helmets.

The final leg with my now well-known band of 30 was a train from Pusan to Seoul. The train journey was pretty grim after all the travelling and battle training we had undergone. It was November, it was cold. No Heating on the train and initially no food or water for the soldiers. After a bit of a fuss we managed to extract 35 one-day ration packs from the US movements system and a crate of Coca Cola. The journey itself was immensely depressing; the railway tracks were littered with apparently starving Korean children who had been displaced during the toing and froing of the war. Then on through the completely desolated countryside by truck to the front just south of the River Imjin.

6

Korea

I had arrived in this war-torn land. The land of "Morning Calm"! Following the end of World War II, Korea was divided into two countries, North and South.

This was formalised in 1948 by division at the 38th parallel – in the North, the Democratic People's Republic of Korea, in the South, the Republic of Korea. The North invaded the South on 25th June 1950. The Security Council of the UN authorised a UN Command to send forces to Korea.

By August 1950, US forces and the South Korean Army were on the brink of defeat. The Pusan perimeter held out.

In September 1950, General MacArthur launched his devastating attack from Inchon and subsequently advanced to the Yalu River on the border with China.

In October 1950, Chinese forces entered Korea. There followed two years of attrition and vicious fighting. Seoul, the capital of South Korea, changed hands four times.

A truce was declared at the end of July 1953. Still no formal Peace, but an end, hopefully, to the most destructive war in the modern era. Three million war dead.

The British contribution was based on the considerable sacrifices in turn of the 27th, 28th, and 29th British Brigades as part of 1st Commonwealth Division.

Following the truce, there were some changes in the operational line of defence (the Kansas line). American and Commonwealth forces re-established the line a touch further south of the Imjin River. A demilitarised zone of approximately 3,000 metres was set up between the two sides. The Allied line was eventually solid from West Coast to East Coast along the 38 parallel. No Korean civilians were permitted within 5,000 metres of the Allied front. All farming remained in abeyance in the combat zone. It was agreed that limited numbers of South Korean troops could remain with Allied forces; these were known as KATCOMS.

The Author, aged 21, on the Kansas Line, Korea 1953

Let me describe my feelings on arrival at the Battalion's location after a journey that had lasted months. There was nobody to be seen! It was a cold Korean November day, late in the afternoon. Nothing moved, no birdsong. The desolate but rugged countryside seemed to have stopped breathing.

Having got my bearings and noted one or two large tin-roofed Quonset huts, I was met by the two Davids! David Bryce-Smith, and David Catmur. They were very welcoming and said we would be living together in their 'hoochie'. "How are you with paddy fields?" "No problem" said I with ridiculous confidence. Gingerly we navigated the paddy bunds, about 18 inches wide and a foot or two above the black-looking water on either side which previously had been planted with rice.

We arrived at our house in the ground. It was a canvas tent that had been dug about 5 feet into the ground. A wooden floor and side walls were a carpenter's dream. Clearly there were spaces for three camp beds, homemade shelves and strings for hanging kit. Lighting by courtesy of Tilly lamps, water by Jerrican and, above all, heating by highly volatile fuel channelled into a fat round boiler. In those halcyon days of peace on the line this was clearly 5-star living!

That first evening I was taken to the Officers' Mess by my companions. The Mess was one of very few Quonset huts. It was furnished entirely by self-made wooden tables and chairs – the wood was recycled from NAAFI boxes of supplies.

The ebullient and charming Commanding Officer, Lt Col Mike Melville was very welcoming and a round of introductions, each with a fresh whisky followed. I now fully understand the two Davids' concern about my familiarity with Paddy fields: to get from the Mess to bed in a hole in the ground, in the dark, full of whisky, along a ¼ mile of Paddy bund was a very daunting and haunting experience.

Work on the new Kansas line of defence had begun in August 1953. I went to my platoon's operational location two days after arrival having been kitted out and fulfilled various administrative chores.

Mortar Detachment, Korea 1953

In layout my impression was nothing has changed since World War I: bunkers connected by endless trenches most of which were strongly revetted. My little platoon headquarters could accommodate 4 of us. Being new and enthusiastic, I quickly realised the dangers of trying to do, or change too much too quickly. There was a well-tried programme of reconstruction that all were used to. To be fussing over much as to whether we were ready if the Chinese launched an attack, via tunnels, tomorrow seemed out of order. Nevertheless, it kept me on my toes and perhaps my 30+ Jocks too!

Apart from improvement to our hillside positions, much training went on. A memorable event was a Company march we did to Inchon; it took 3 days and was a mere 170 miles away. We carried all our weapons and kit and slept by the roadside in sleeping bags with boots still firmly on. It is a sad fact that many American soldiers were to die trapped in sleeping bags with neither quick-release clips nor boots.

The monotony of deep cold, testing training and construction were alleviated for all by a Rest and Recuperation (R&R) trip to Tokyo or Inchon. There were not many takers for Inchon!

One of the few moments I do recall about my spell of R&R was the immediacy of a sudden arrival by air near Tokyo and then being whisked to a luxury Forces Leave hotel. Imagine, a bed, clean linen, Japanese bath, and any number of attractive young Japanese girls who dealt with your laundry, your mail – how to phone home, etc.

Regrettably, I never saw Tokyo by day. We played by night, returned to the hotel to find laundry done, snacks and hot drinks available, and so to bed! After a few days I was happy to fly back to Korea – for a touch of R&R!

7

Canal Zone, Egypt

By June 1954, our tour in Korea was complete. We were bound for Suez for six months to complete a full overseas tour. We embarked on the troopship Empire Fowey with short stopovers in Hong Kong, Singapore, and Colombo. What an excitement for a 21-year-old. Just to ensure we kept the tempo going, Bob Richardson (senior subaltern, to go on to be GOC Northern Ireland) and I decided to put on a cabaret before we reached Egypt. What to do? In 1954, the Andrews Sisters were still just memorable. We had the tapes for music but what about dresses, hats, etc? Quite a testing problem on a troopship

'The Andrews Sisters' – with Lt Bob Richardson (right)

loaded with soldiers overburdened with testosterone. It so happened there were three army nurses onboard. Bob and I were tall and lean and with the required amount of squeezing, looked pretty shapely!

The cabaret went well, even if there were on or two derisory comments! Sadly, we were unable to return the dresses in the immaculate order they were lent to us. We made our apologies and thanks to these sporting young nurses.

We disembarked at Suez in mid-July 1954. There was an ongoing crisis in political leadership at the time we arrived in Egypt. In summary, the Colonels Naguib and Nasser staged a coup d'état in 1952; in July 1952 King Farouk sailed into exile to Italy; in July 1953, General Naguib became the first President of Egypt; Colonel Nasser became Prime Minister in November having dismissed Naguib as President. Nasser became President of Egypt in 1956. At the time, British Forces based in the Canal Zone were not too troubled by Egyptian politics. Security of the canal was all important. Little were we to know what was to come!

The site for our accommodation was a strip of desert with some old EPIP (Indian Army) tents flapping in the oil-laden wind. There were bundles of other tents strewn around. This tented site was overrun by feral cats. The cats were duly despatched, and a big tidy up programme began.

Shortly after we settled in, Bob Richardson and I were sent to receive and escort the Regimental Colours from Port Said to Suez. The Colours had remained in Scotland during the tour in Korea. We duly arrived in Port Said by truck after a long and dusty journey. Bob hailed a military Movements Officer in the dockyard and told him we were there to collect the Colours of The Royal Scots. He, the Movements Officer, stared blankly back as only someone in that trade can do when there are unstoppable and unreasonable delays to movement!

Out of the corner of our eyes we watched as a long black crate was lowered by crane to the dockside. Clearly our Colours. As the crate swung perilously above the filthy dock water, Bob and I wondered if we could survive our careers watching the Colours submerge in Port Said waters. All was well and we had two full quaichs of whisky on return.

The environs of Suez town were singularly unattractive. The whole area was pervaded by the stink of oil and its derivatives. The town was 'Off Limits' to British troops – not something we wept about! We were to be in Suez for six months before returning home to the UK. Our task was to protect the oil installations – that apart, the desert was ours in which to train. New skills were acquired such as navigation by sun compass. For some of course, the sun never shined!

Excitement for some was provided by the restaurant over the canal run by Nellie, Fifi and Zsa Zsa, three Arab ladies who defied the 'Off Limits' rules and provided good food and music. We knew the place well and had our escape route planned in case of a Military Police raid. One evening, to our complete surprise, a Major from the Regiment walked in. We enjoyed drinks together and warned him of the possibility of a Military Police raid. Sure enough – sirens off stage. We tucked the Major under the full-length tablecloth and made our escape via a hatch and garage door. To our utter dismay, the Major was seen next morning leaving the Commanding Officer's office looking a touch hangdog!

The Commanding Officer at the time was Lt Col Bill Campbell CBE. I was lucky enough to be the only subaltern to serve with him throughout his extraordinary active tour in command. Bill Campbell was much exercised by our next move to the UK. First it was to be Dover, but this changed to Elgin. The next rumour was Cyprus, then confirmation it was to be Elgin. Finally, a signal that we were to move at short notice to Cyprus!!

Just imagine the implications of this apparent Ministry of Defence (MOD) incompetence. We had advance parties in Dover, Elgin, and Cyprus, all from Egypt, to make our next unit move smoother!

It was now two years on since the unit had left Scotland for Korea. When would families reunite and where? In the event another six months of separation with an emergency tour in Cyprus.

8

Cyprus 1955–56

Extremists supporting 'Enosis' Union with Greece formed EOKA. Col Grivas led EOKA and began a campaign of terror in Cyprus in late 1955. At one stage, about 20,000 British troops were seeking Grivas and the British Colonial Administration offered a reward of £10,000 for information leading to an arrest. We never caught him, and he was finally to die a 75-year-old fugitive in a hideout near the southern port of Limassol.

Coral Bay was, in 1955, in its natural state. There was not a villa to be seen, nor indeed any Cypriot restaurant or coffee house. The battalion headquarters and all the ancillary logistic departments were to set up at Coral Bay, including the main cookhouse and Officers' Mess, etc. Some sites required hard concrete bases, and these were quickly done by the Cyprus Public Works Department (PWD). Signs of concrete bases puzzle tourists today.

Security was very tight as Coral Bay was not too distant from Khlorakas where Grivas was reported to have come ashore by rowing boat from Greece. The battalion was part of 3 Commando Brigade based in Paphos District employed wholly on anti-terrorist operations.

I found myself in a base at Stroumbi; a delightful Greek/Turkish Cypriot village with a volcanic record and a remarkable red wine. Despite the friendliness of the villagers, one had to be constantly alert against acts of terrorism.

Previously and for some time thereafter, there were many violent shootings in the main shopping area of Nicosia, Ledra Street. The targets, many fatal, were European women and children, and of course soldiers. The Cypriot police were corrupt and inefficient and did not really contribute to the fight against terrorism.

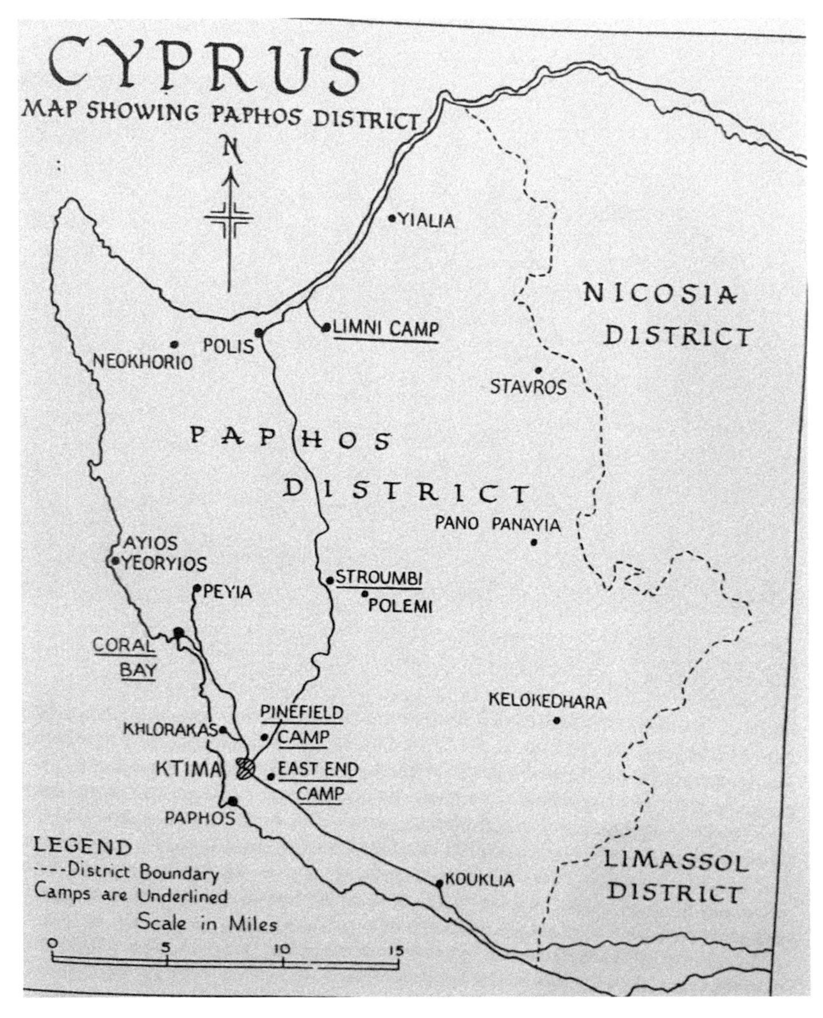

Cyprus, September 1955 – January 1956 1st Battalion, The Royal Scots
Reproduced from The Thistle, May 1956, and A History of The Royal Scots (Vol 2)

The urban threat quickly spilled over into the countryside. It was complicated by the harmonious relations at village level between Greek and Turkish Cypriots turning sour; to the extent of driving the latter out of shared villages.

In the large rural area with which we were concerned, we were full time cordoning off villages in the search for weapons, explosives, and wanted men. Continuous vigilance was required against ambush at any time on the narrow tortuous roads. Our vehicles gave little protection.

One of the more difficult spots in our area was the village of Polis. There was a large village school, seemingly coping with all ages – the whole very pro Enosis. Thus, the scene was set for many a riot with women and small children in the front ranks covering assorted teenage rock throwers who in turn covered the more dangerous terrorist element. Such illegal assemblies occurred regularly and were difficult to deal with. In 1955–56 the British Army's arms and legs were bound by legal procedures covering dispersal of crowds/riots.

A more pleasant diversion was to the centre of the Cyprus tin-mining industry at Limni. Ore had been mined in the Polis/Limni area since Roman times. In the 1940s, an outage of 500 tons a day was planned. During our tour we were required to provide protection for the Limni mine. A very pleasant duty: managed by an hospitable British team and providing wonderful cool facilities to escape the Cyprus heat.

We had an excellent relationship with the Royal Navy who operated seaborne patrols from minesweepers along the coast in our area from the Akamas peninsula to Paphos. Sailors would come ashore for a game of football, and we had the occasional evening afloat. I recall one evening after a wardroom dinner the Picquet Boat could not be found? We had to swim back into Coral Bay!

After some weeks I was asked to go and see the Commanding Officer. Bill Campbell said "Philip, I have selected you to go to Nicosia as ADC to the Director of Operations, Cyprus". In fact, the job was not much more than one of personal protection. Added bonuses were chances to socialise, and the provision of a military motorbike. The former allowed visits to Kyrenia, where, at the Harbour Club one night, I found myself at a table next to Ava Gardner! The motorbike, less voluptuous, was to move important messages to important people in the city. How grateful I was for that compulsory motorcycle training at Sandhurst. On a more daunting note, I was summoned one day by the Secretariat and invited to turn the billiard room at Government House into map and operations rooms. The arrival of Field Marshal, Sir John Harding, as the new Governor of Cyprus was imminent. I was not familiar with the build of a full-size billiard table but basically, they are made of sheets of heavy slate. To move two tables out of the room was a prodigious task.

After many hours, four walls in the new map room were suitably adorned. I awaited the Field Marshal's verdict. He was satisfied.

All good things come to an end and my lasting image of Cyprus 1955–56 was that of Bill Campbell driving his Land Rover at speed with pipe clamped in mouth, one hand on the radio microphone and the other on a map – who was steering?!

Thus, ended my first real experience of anti-terrorism operations. An experience that was to be repeated time and again in the remaining years.

9

Scottish Interlude

We left Limassol in January 1956 having handed over to 40 Commando. We arrived in England early February and went up to Elgin, Scotland by train. Pinefield Camp was to be our new home, but first for all was some leave and of course, reunion with families separated for nearly three years.

I believe our mission in Scotland was to enjoy life free of any operational contingencies. That was certainly the impression given by the General Officer Commanding (GOC) Scotland when he visited the Battalion shortly after our arrival.

Peace time soldiering in Scotland was outwardly pretty relaxed. Fishing (The Spey), shooting and golf. Look under the carpet and there was a pile of guard duties, honour guards, Retreat programmes, range work, etc, etc. At the time, Elgin was a very agreeable city; used to soldiers and welcoming. The area was filled with distilleries – some of the best Macallan on the Spey, and Aberlour not far away.

We had a very good social and sporting relationship with the Royal Naval Air Station (RNAS) at Lossiemouth. The distinguished Captain Gick RN and Bill Campbell put together a covert plan for the Battalion to test as realistically as possible the security of RNAS.

I was given the task of putting together a night raid. We got prepared, blackened up, weapons loaded with blank ammo, smoke grenades and finally homemade sticky bombs to attach to RNAS aircraft.

We approached the site on foot at about 2am. We cut through the perimeter wire and not a sound to be heard. The first of our bombers moved silently towards the aircraft and positioned sticky grenades. Then, suddenly all hell was let loose, sirens, lights, and Alsatian dogs with handlers. Captain Gick had been true to his word – the station thought this was for real. Many of us were rounded up and flung into cells, buckets or bags on heads. We were not treated kindly but eventually a truce was called. Captain Gick was later to write to Bill Campbell a warm letter of thanks and congratulations.

Our stay in Elgin seemed thoroughly secure – that is until President Nasser, on 26th July 1956 nationalised the Suez Canal. In early August, seven days' notice to move to the Middle East was imposed. Shortly afterwards, several hundred Reservists were called up and re-joined the Battalion. They arrived long-haired and angry at possibly losing their jobs and being separated from family.

Haircuts, some firm words and much re-training and they were quickly back in shape. An invaluable contribution without which we could not have coped. In August 1956, at seven days' notice still, we moved to Bodney Camp, Norfolk for battle training. All our vehicles were taken away for loading at Southampton Docks.

Despite the seven days' notice to move, we were in Norfolk for another two months: on training humping all our kit including support weapons on our backs. I had little doubt that we were off to war in Egypt. I therefore decided to seek permission from the CO to get married (25 years old before marriage was allowed in the Army in the 1950s). I had met Mona, my wife to be, in the Canal Zone in 1954. She was a Nursing Sister with the RAF. Colonel Bill readily assented with the proviso I was to be back in Norfolk within 72 hours!

Not surprisingly, there were one or two little administrative problems facing me. All my kit and my car were in Elgin; unlike some smart units, who go to war with Dinner Jacket and perhaps Morning Suit at the ready, I was naked for the pending ceremony in St Giles. Jo Forbes insisted I borrow a well-cut dark suit of his and Archie Addison offered to drive me up to Edinburgh from Norfolk with a Great Dane puppy on my lap – a sister for his great love, Portia. I subsequently used the Land Rover to get back to Norfolk on time. Put a 3″ mortar base plate on my back and resume training with the Mortar Platoon.

Mona very sportingly agreed to arrange everything in Edinburgh where she was doing private nursing, in King Street. She had been nursing Doctor Charles Warr, the Queen's Chaplain in Scotland. He agreed to marry us on 25th August 1956 in the Chapel of Youth within St Giles' Cathedral. A one-night honeymoon at Greywalls Hotel in Gullane and back to Norfolk alone! In early November we embarked on our old friend Empire Fowey. Next stop Port Said?

10

Suez Operation

In July 1956, President Gamal Abdel Nasser nationalised the Suez Canal.

Following protracted secret negotiations between Israeli, French and British governments, a plot was hatched. Israel was to attack in the Sinai desert followed by an ultimatum from Britain and France for a cease fire. This was ignored. Britain and France landed paratroops on 5th November. Egyptian forces were rapidly defeated, but they had successfully blocked the Canal to all shipping.

Parachute landings were followed by seaborne landings on 6th November. At which time we were off Malta listening to the BBC saying a cease fire had been agreed. We eventually disembarked on 14th November taking over from 45 Commando. It has to be said that this operational arrival and this disembarkation in a warzone could have come from the brilliant Ealing Film Studios:-

11TH NOVEMBER 1956

GUARDSHIP TO MASTER OF EMPIRE FOWEY:- "WHY ARE YOU NOT PROCEEDING?"

MASTER:- "NO ORDERS TO PROCEED"

GUARDSHIP:-"PROCEED TO HARBOUR IMMEDIATELY, UP ANCHOR, AND MOVE ALONGSIDE"

HMS TRAFALGAR:- "YOU ARE NOT WANTED YET. TURN AROUND AND RETURN TO ANCHORAGE"!!

On the 14th of November 1956, we landed with pretty mixed and frustrated feelings. Our main responsibility was security within the Arab Quarter of Port Said and some peripheral port areas. The situation buzzed day and night like an angry hornets' nest. That apart, the USA was threatening economic action against the United Kingdom unless we withdrew and accepted a takeover by UN Forces.

The humiliating position was that British and French forces had successfully moved 30km south either side of the Canal thus overcoming adjacent marshland, Thereafter Suez was in sight and the desert open for armour. I found myself down at El Cap for a short time and met some interesting French Foreign Legionnaires from England, Ireland, USA, Germany, etc.

To return to our area of interest. A curfew 6pm to 6am was established. Meetings over ten persons had to be dispersed. There were constant demands from the locals for medical aid and fires were a constant hazard. Patrolling on foot and by vehicle was never ending and quite hazardous. In a tragic incident, a patrol led by Major David Pinkerton MC was ambushed and he subsequently died of his wounds. There is little doubt such actions were driven by drugged Egyptian soldiers. On arrival in the Arab Quarter, we had seen much Egyptian uniform and equipment dropped in the streets and, surprise, surprise, a lot of healthy young men wandering about in gleaming white djellabas.

Before leaving the scented Arab Quarter, the ghastly problem of sewerage should not be forgotten. The Assault Pioneers led by Alan Mitchell-Innes were given the problem to crack. Typically leading from the front, without any protective clothing, he disappeared down the sewer shaft. Day after day of relentless work which I do not believe was ever properly recognised.

In mid-December 1956, we handed over our positions to a UN-badged battalion of the Swedish Army. This was not an especially

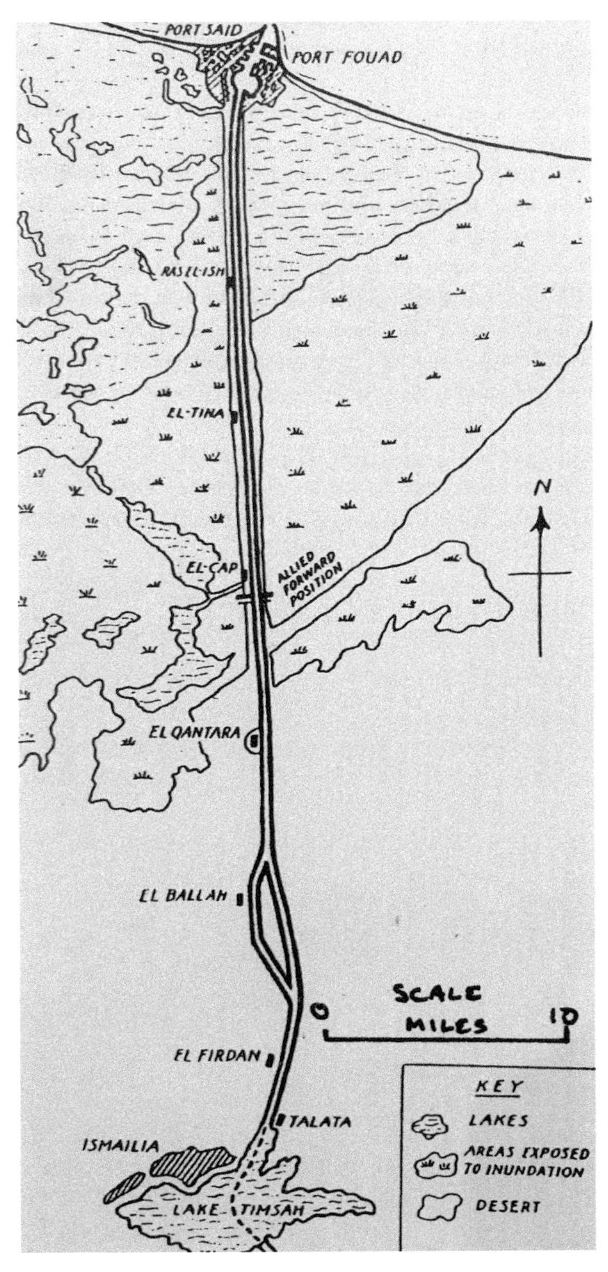

The Suez Operation, 1956
Reproduced from The Thistle, May 1957, and A History of The Royal Scots (Vol 2)

friendly affair. We were thwarted and frustrated; the jack-booted Swedes displayed a touch of almost Germanic arrogance. No doubt both sides were at fault.

Later that week we embarked on the troopship Dunera bound for Southampton. The last troopship to leave Port Said. Christmas and New Year were celebrated aboard HMT Dunera although festive spirit was in short supply because the ship was very overcrowded, rations were short, and the weather was foul!

11

UK – On The Move

By train back to Elgin, and Pinefield Camp. Two memorable events before we all went on a month's leave' firstly, we thanked and discharged our splendid Reservists; second, I met with my new wife, Mona, last seen six months previously for 24 hours!

During 1957 in Elgin, we were back to the endless provision of Honour Guards and many extra mural activities. The Regiment was also privileged to be invited to provide the Royal Guard for HM The Queen at Balmoral. I was lucky enough to go on the Guard as one of three subalterns under the command of Major Alastair MacGeorge MC.

One of many experiences I had at Ballater was an invitation from HM The Queen to go stalking. The drill was that one met up with the Stalker on a lawn in the grounds. A wooden target had been positioned for one to take a couple of sighting shots into the lower shoulder. Assuming all went well the two of you set off. Let us be clear one was very much under the advice and admonition of the Stalker.

The approach to the selected stag was an electric moment. Then settle down, deep breaths and do not wound the beast. You have probably walked several miles over the hills, splashed along and indeed crawled through many streams. Now hold your breath, steady, and shoot to kill!

The pony man takes the carcass away and one goes with the Stalker to his cottage – if invited! I was given a cup of tea and biscuits in the front room and then happily joined up with the family in the kitchen. I was very fortunate to receive a further invitation from HM The Queen for another day's stalking.

I was to leave Elgin in late autumn 1957. During the ten months or so spent there we had two houses to live in. I was not yet 25 years old and there were no military Quarters available anyway.

Very generously, Major George Dunlop MC and his wife, Aileen put us up for some weeks. Subsequently we rented our first marital home just outside Elgin. Number 1, Institution Road, Elgin! I mention this because we almost lost count of houses occupied during my time in the army. We shall keep count.

We are now off to Eaton Hall Officer Cadet School (OCS) near Chester where I am to be an Instructor. I am pleased because I much enjoyed my experience as a cadet at Eaton Hall. Also, it balanced out a previous posting to Netheravon as a Support Weapons Instructor which was not ratified. Suddenly, there was a need for Gurkhali speakers! (Malayan Emergency?).

Once more there was no army quarter available. My wife and I found Coombe Dale Lodge at Bickerton, a few miles from Eaton Hall.

Teaching basic tactics to potential young infantry officers was extremely rewarding. The cadets were as keen as mustard and the whole system was geared up to promote leadership in its many forms.

In 1958 Eaton Hall OCS merged with Mons OCS in Aldershot. Before our move south to Mons OCS we celebrated the birth of our first child, Jacqueline, born in Chester. Mons OCS was not Eaton Hall and Aldershot was not Chester. Enough said! Once more, no army quarter so we found another hiring.

Mons OCS now became the only establishment training potential national service officers for all arms. One never quite knew whether the steady old Cavalry and Gunner cadets resented the arrival of exuberant infantry cadets. Of course, many lasting friendships were made. I recall a certain officer cadet, Michael Heseltine, in my Company. He appeared ambitious both to "get on" and to "get out". He succeeded! Call-ups for National Service ended in December 1960 and the last National Servicemen left the Armed Forces in 1963. As a young regular officer, I saw the whole system through. In part a sausage machine but one that turned boys into men. Not a pragmatic view but I was and remain a supporter.

In June 1958, my brother David married Ann (nee Farquharson) at Brompton Oratory with a reception at the Savoy. Ann's father, Duncan had served with the Garhwal Rifles during the Burma Campaign. Ann and David subsequently had three children, Iain, Angela, and Jennifer. After a fight of some years against cancer, Ann slipped her mooring peacefully surrounded by her family in December 2008. David passed away ten years later.

My family and I left Aldershot in the early autumn of 1959 to re-join the Battalion coming to the end of their tour in Berlin. We were allocated our first army quarter. Guards and ceremonial were the order of the day in Berlin. Within the British sector there was neither the real estate nor the scope for exercises above sub unit level. On the other hand, the city provided plenty of opportunity for enjoyment and my wife and I were able to do in three months what it had taken many to do in two years.

The rumour machine operated to the full in this city of spies. At one time the Regiment was off to Aden, the next time Benghazi. In the event we were to move, in February 1960, to Troon, Ayrshire by train from Berlin.

We arrived at Dundonald Camp extremely weary after a 17-hour train journey. On arrival, the Jocks were properly cared for but not withstanding the efforts of the housing staff, many of us were "moved in" at night to Quarters with walls and bedding streaming with damp and totally unwelcoming. The military system at its very worst.

Some leave for all followed and Lt Col Peter Maxwell took over command from Lt Col David McQueen DSO. I was fortunate to be appointed Adjutant of the battalion at this time. I recall there was much to be done. A visit by HRH The Princess Royal in August followed by detailed planning of a unit move to Benghazi in October 1960.

12
Libya

Libya gained Independence under King Idris in 1961. At the time, the British Government called in a Treaty of Friendship with Libya. In exchange for economic aid, the British Government secured continuing use of British bases in Cyrenaica.

Our arrival in Libya in October 1960 was a test of nerve and resources. The main body of the unit was lifted to Tobruk on HMT Dunera. Further movement of equipment and troops by Landing Ships Tanks (LSTs) to Benghazi. Many flights, mostly families by RAF air trooping to RAF El Adem. Then buses and vehicles onwards.

In all, about 600 soldiers and 200 wives and children were to survive the move from Scotland to Libya without mishap. The new base, Wavell Barracks was tented but fairly quickly converted to huts. We found a hiring above the Casino in Benghazi as there was no quarter available. We were eventually rehoused to a new flat nearer the Barracks.

In 1960, Benghazi was primitive, dirty, corrupt, and of course Arab as opposed to Italian. There was, however, a kind of endearment between the town Arabs and the British soldiers – perhaps a relic of the last war when we were in and out of Tobruk/Benghazi like a volleyball.

I recall trying to clear my new Renault Dauphin car through Customs. Every effort was put in by Customs Officers to obtain a backhander. No bribe, no car!

This game went on over weeks until the authorities ran out of ideas for further delays such as wrong documentation, wrong specification, etc.

The Benghazi Casino, above which we found a tiny apartment for the three of us was in what might be called a salubrious spot in the town. It had a tiny kitchen, complete with primus stove for cooking. Mona never complained, although the prospect of cooking Christmas lunch on a primus stove was a challenge too far, and the Officers Mess, about a mile away in a lovely old stable block, came to the rescue. They sent down by truck a roasted chicken with all the trimmings.

I am not an addictive gambler, but it did occur to me that one should make best use of the facilities available to us. We therefore happily agreed that I could have a casino evening once a week with a spending limit of £5! As with all gambling, sometimes I walked upstairs to the apartment having doubled my money – sometimes not!

Once we were settled down there were huge opportunities to learn how to operate in the desert. Not least navigation using the sun compass or the stars. There were to be desert expeditions and countless exercises which in some cases revisited World War II battlefields such as Mechili. A particular exercise took place in and around the desert battlefield of Mechili, where stricken tank hulls still lay as did wire entanglements with red triangular tin labels marked "Achtung Minen".

Our 'enemy' on this occasion were the Black Watch part of 3 Brigade over from Cyprus for desert training. The two regiments, one Highland and one Lowland, were blessed with a friendly disposition but of course in reality were keen rivals. Edward Cowan, temporarily leading the Reconnaissance platoon of The Royal Scots worked his way into the 'battle' positions of the Black Watch which sharpened them up a touch. We also locked onto their formation

Briefing for an exercise

Troops moving in the desert

radio frequency which allowed us to disrupt, for a very short time, their plans for attack. In summary, a thoroughly good and realistic exercise. I suppose above all it brought home to us what toughness, discipline and fearlessness had been exercised by soldiers of the VIII Army in the desert 1941–43.

The Palace, Tripoli

The Suk in Murzuk

A grass Tibu hut, in the desert south of Tripoli

One of the most ambitious expeditions was led by Francis Gibb to the Tibesti Mountains on the border with Chad. As military expeditions go, this one was not just ambitious, but testing, with vehicle problems in the sand, heat, and a huge distance to cover, and water supply and radio contact throughout.

Subject to shifts in political clearance, I believe the aim was to get as close as possible to Emi Koussi (4-430m), the barren volcano in the heart of the Sahara Desert and close to the Libyan border.

For some months prior to the start date of the expedition, there had been discussion between London and Libyan/British authorities as to the participation of Randolph Churchill. He, apparently, insisted on shipping his own Land Rover and indeed later on special radio equipment had to be shipped so that he was in constant touch with Westminster!

Came the day after huge amounts of nagging officialdom, the great man arrived at the Officers Mess just outside Benghazi. That night, the day before the expedition set off, we had a Guest Night in the Mess for Mr Churchill. I recall he appeared looking fresh, slightly flushed, and smart in a dinner jacket. It was not long into dinner before the jacket came off and there was Winston's son in his red braces holding forth!

The expedition leaves commanded by Francis Gibb. Apocryphal it may be, but some doubt was expressed about who was to lead? It was not long into that first day that Randolph Churchill had a problem with water rationing or his communications. All turned back. Day two was going well, but Mr Churchill was not enjoying the heat and apparently had lost communication with Westminster via his special radio system. Mr Churchill turned back again and returned to London. It only goes to say that after a trying start, out of his hands, Francis led a highly successful expedition to the Tibesti Mountains.

It was in a temperature of 100° that my wife set about giving birth to our second daughter at the British Military Hospital near Benghazi. To this day, living in Florida and married to an American, Jane suffers from the endorsement on her passport "born in Benghazi, Libya".

I was 700 miles away at the time, in Tripoli, sitting the Staff College entry exam. Three days of written papers in those days! Of course, there was an exam setter's failure in one paper which caused justifiable consternation! The paper in question, Tactics, was invalidated or we were all given a pass mark?

I returned to Benghazi to see Mona delivered of a baby girl, Stephanie-Jane, a sister for Jackie. The sun and climate seemed to suit Jackie. Jane was much fairer, and time would tell if she liked hot climates! Both clearly enjoyed the Mediterranean sea. We had a young Arab boy as a make-do gardener. He was delightful and got on well with the girls. To see Hassan and Jackie in a tiny patch of garden was a treat. He was teaching her to sow egg plant seeds which would grow into loofahs to scrub your back!

As Adjutant of the battalion, one was also President of The Pipes and Drums. The Cyrenaican Police had an embryo Pipe Band which was short of a Tartan! My wife and I duly went down to the

Souk in Benghazi to see if we could solve the problem. The Souk was swimming in tartan! We chose an Ancient Lindsay which was received with much joy by the Libyan pipers!

Within the year we were on the move again, 700 miles up the road to Tripoli. Before departing the very likeable Arab town of Benghazi we felt obliged to inflict a final burst of British Culture and with the aid of the British Council we performed A Midsummer Night's Dream in Benghazi Zoo Gardens.

Performance in English but with scripts for the audience in Arabic. A well-received evening! I recall Edward Cowan in a leading role. Inevitably I was one of the Clowns/Bottom?

We arrived in Tripoli during October in good order with two young daughters. Tripoli was very cosmopolitan with strong Italian influence. We were given a delightful Italian villa to live in. Our house in Georgimpopouli was probably lived in by a smart Italian family in the days when Italy were colonial rulers.

The Officers Club, shops, and restaurants were all very conveniently placed. If we went out to a restaurant it would be lunchtime because in everlasting Italian style, nobody eats before 10pm in the evening. Mona bought all our food locally and used the market a lot – abundant with fruit from the fertile land north and south of Derna.

A very pleasant American Service family lived bang opposite us. Sadly, they seemed to have a repetitive illness problem within the family however, we eventually discovered it was almost self-inflicted. They did not shop locally, either for food or water, but bought everything including crates of water from the PX store at the American air force base, Wheelus Field, a few kilometres outside Tripoli.

The Jocks were happily in a proper Italian barracks and enjoyed the more Mediterranean lifestyle in Tripoli.

13

Staff College – One Malaysia

Towards the end of the year, I had heard that I had passed the exam and been selected for Staff College. Entry to Staff College was now by way of a three-month course at the Royal Military College of Science (RMCS) Shrivenham. A daunting prospect for a non-scientific infantier! The course assembled in late September 1962.

We left the many good friends we had made in Tripoli and headed back home by air in the summer of 1962. A brief pitstop with parents and then to search for a house that would suit three months at Shrivenham and a year at Camberley. We found a hiring near Camberley.

RMCS was very convivial. I was one of many weekly commuters. I regret to say that much of the content of the course went straight over my head. We were, of course, at this time in the midst of the worsening Cuban missile crisis. There were good reasons to be distracted.

Christmas 1962 with the family and then the Camberley year. The winter of 1962/63 was horrific to the extent that we had frozen windows in and outside, burst pipes, etc. We had to move quickly and once again no Quarter was available. We found a cosy house in Camberley.

I was lucky enough to be centred on Minley Manor, the more gentrified part of Staff College. The year at Camberley was at a fast pace and all-consuming. Strategy to tactics to logistics all fought over in small syndicates led by a Lt Col of the Directing Staff. Visits to industry, battlefield tours, and many, many, diverse locations.

Some long-lasting friendships were formed, not least with overseas students. Several relationships were particularly useful when one met up on an overseas tour.

Postings from Camberley were made known in late-November. I was off to Malaysia as Staff Officer to the newly appointed Director of the recently raised Malaysia Rangers. Colonel Wellsted was based in Singapore and the Rangers were at the Gurkha Depot in Sungei Patani, northern Malaya.

I had business to do in Singapore before going north. We decided my wife and the two girls should go ahead and stay in Kuala Lumpur with friends. All went well. We joined up in KL and went on by rail north. Once again, there was no question of a military quarter in Sungei Patani. A very generous officer in the 7th Gurkha Rifles agreed to put us up for a few weeks while we looked for accommodation.

Life in Sungei Patani was quintessentially a life of the colonial past, but with a deep undercurrent of the need for professionalism to meet the threat past and present of incursion by communist terrorists.

The working day began in the Gurkha Mess at 6am with a wonderful bowl of mulligatawny soup (Gurkha style), follow by fresh sliced pineapple or mango, followed by bacon and eggs, etc.

Concentrated work from 7am until noon; this might entail jungle craft, navigation, fitness training, or, most important of all, weapon training. The Gurkha soldier had to be totally at one with his weapon whether it be a Kukri knife, rifle, or machine gun. He was trained to strip weapons in the dark, get them into action, change hot barrels blind-folded, etc.

Lunchtime, normally a very light meal in the week, but at the weekends, the Plantation curry event would occur. There would be an exodus by invitation to the neighbouring Rubber Estates. Several Tiger beers later you would be tucking into curry of a like not to be found anywhere else – explosively hot, but irresistible.

On one occasion, at a curry lunch, I remember the CO of the Depot teasing Mona – "he had a Dutch wife", he said, "and kept cool by putting her between his legs". Mona's eyes were out on stalks! The 'Dutch Wife' was, of course, a bolster!

I was the only Staff Officer working between the Director and the Commanding Officers of the two Ranger battalions: Lt Col Edward 'Fairy' Gopsill and Lt Col David Woods. Why 'Fairy' Gopsill? He was huge, tough as old iron and highly decorated. Probably a Gurkha nickname of much respect. All the officers in the units were British. The concept of the Malaysian Rangers was based on the increasing confrontation between Indonesia and the Malaysian states of Sabah and Sarawak. There was a demand for deployment of more jungle trackers. In particular, the Ibans of Sarawak were highly skilled. A recruitment plan was devised to recruit trackers in Sabah and Sarawak and subsequently train them at the Gurkha depot at Sungei Patani. The training was similar to that given to Gurkha recruits enlisted from up country Nepal. Many days learning to cope with boots and laces followed by intensive weapon training.

It was not too long, about six weeks before we were offered a house on the jungle edge at the perimeter of the camp. We snatched it up. House number 13. The children loved the newfound freedom and conversations with wandering iguanas. In due course, the girls attended a Malay/Chinese School. They were the two objects of curiosity and never looked back!

It was inevitable that the newly formed Rangers would outgrow their stay with the Gurkhas. The move was south to new barracks at Ipoh. We hit the jackpot this time and were immediately offered a delightful hiring within metres of the Officers' Club which had a good-sized swimming pool. Before heading south, we took the opportunity to take a cool leave break with the girls in the Cameron Highlands; a delightful hill station comprising a few bungalows, a nine-hole golf course, and many footpaths into the surrounding jungle. Naturally we invented many tigers in the jungle (there had been a recent scare) and fun was had by all running like mad from imaginary beasts.

Life in Ipoh was exhilarating compared to the heat and stickiness of Sungei Patani. We were now very much part of the British military community in Ipoh. Cricket, rugby, and racing at Ipoh racecourse; not to mention curry lunches on the Rubber Estates. In late 1964, I had news of a new posting. It was to be Assistant Military Attaché (Army) at the British High Commission in Kuala Lumpur. I was to take over the appointment from Major Mig Witt RA. He and his wife, Fizz were delightful and immediately invited us all to stay in their High Commission house until the handover of work was complete. During this period, we were lucky enough to inherit many of their friends from Embassies around the world.

The Military Attaché to the High Commissioner, Sir Anthony Head, was Colonel Lewis who in turn was served by three assistant service attachés. The work was not onerous but absorbing with the situation of confrontation in Borneo. Antony Head was a delight to work for along with his Deputy, James Bottomley – the father of Sir Henry Bottomley MP.

Kuala Lumpur was a bit of a social whirl for the family. A car and chauffeur were available for work. We joined the Royal Selangor Golf Club where vast sums of money were played for on the golf courses as well as diplomatic deals being made. I used to play a bit of tennis; this was handy as I was periodically blown for by the High Commissioner to partner him against the Chinese at Carcosa. He nearly ran into a

Lord Head, High Commissioner of Malaya

little local trouble as he never played tennis with Malays. The two girls, meanwhile, would spend many afternoons swimming at the Selangor Club. Their mother had arranged swimming lessons with a retired lady Olympic swimmer. The pair of them became really strong swimmers.

There was also the duty to host and attend many diplomatic parties from the huge number of Missions in KL. Mona, one evening helping to host a party at Carcosa, the British Residence, spotted two lonely and gloomy-looking men on their own. To the Pakistan High Commissioner "do come with me, there is someone I would like you to meet". He took one look over. "Not for me, madam. That is the Indian High Commissioner. We declared war about an hour ago."! Mona was a delightful diplomatic success. Always caring, smiling, and looking good. One long, boring diplomatic drinks party she really got stuck with an elderly and tedious retired American Admiral. Like a butterfly she is suddenly free and joins another group saying "Hello, how good to see you. I've just been stuck with a very boring old Admiral". "Oh, you must mean by brother-in-law", replies her new-found friend!

It was in early 1966 that I heard my next posting was to re-join The Royal Scots in Osnabrück, Germany. Although I had done German language at school, that was by now some time ago. I was determined to see if I could find a teacher in KL. In the event, I enrolled at the Goethe Institute in KL for a German conversation course. I have to say that I was amazed at the quality of the course, and I presumed my teacher would be one of the many German expatriates living in KL. Not so, veil lifted she was an attractive Chinese/Malay girl who had taken a degree at Heidelberg University!

We were ready to return to the UK in the summer and were advised by the High Commission Secretariat that we were entitled to a First-Class passage to the UK by ship. How well the Diplomatic Service lived! In the event, we had to fly First Class by Qantas because of a clash with shipping and school dates.

Such apparent extravagance should not go unnoticed. Due to the assorted levels of bureaucracy between Kuala Lumpur and London I did not receive any diplomatic allowances until the last six months of my tour in KL. The post I filled was rated by the Foreign Office as that of a First Secretary in the diplomatic service thus, in my last six months of service in KL, my diplomatic allowance amounted to more than my current basic army pay! The differentials are staggering when the British military philosophy of 'Can do!' – 'Go anywhere!' – 'At any time!' is taken into account.

14

On The Move Again – France One

We arrived at Osnabrück by car in late autumn 1966. We were allotted an excellent German military quarter. Our immediate neighbours were the family of our military doctor, Dr Paul Jackson and his wife, from the Netherlands, Wilhelmina, and their children who were of similar ages to ours.

I took over Support Company. The battalion was equipped with Armoured Personnel Carriers (APCs) based on the Fighting Vehicles 432 (FV432). Much hard training was already under way so that the infantry could work more flexibly with tank units.

Anti-Personnel Carriers in Osnabrück

It seemed that I had hardly been in Osnabrück for five minutes when I was summonsed to see the Commanding Officer, Lt Col Bill Currie. A bit of chit chat "Glad to hear you are all settled in, Philip". "I'm afraid I have a bit of news that may come as a shock", he said. "We have been told to provide an Officer to assemble, to move, to set up, and to run a new Battle Training Maintenance Centre for armoured units of the 1st British Corps, based in Germany. The establishment is to be located near Timimi in the Libyan desert. You have just two months before the Centre is to open. He finished by saying "I will try and ensure you are only committed to the job for six months".

My mind was reeling. Leaving new young family; Mona spoke no German; who do I turn to for advice for this huge and important job.

Help was at hand, and I quickly found myself attached to and working with a very hospitable Gunner unit. With their help a huge amount of heavy equipment was gathered up for shipment from France to Tobruk. This included JCBs, cranes, spare tank engines, tank tracks, etc. That was just some of the hardware. We had to shift tentage and all the ancillaries to build our own camp. It was a mammoth undertaking not least just to find Timini which lay between Benghazi and Tobruk in the shadow of Gebel Akhdar.

I did return to British Army of the Rhine (BAOR) after seven months and was happy to learn that HQ 1st British Corps were very satisfied with the desert training centre. In May 1967, Lt Col David Young assumed Command from Bill Currie. Life continued apace and there was never a dull moment from Exercises, skiing, and many adventure activities.

In the Spring of 1968, off to another staff job as GS02 Intelligence at HQ 3rd Division, Bulford. The General Officer Commanding was General Terence McMeekin. Delightful to work for but extremely energetic. The 21st birthday of his daughter was matched by the christening of a son. The Commander in Chief at the time sent a signal "McMeekin it is clear to me you don't have enough to do!". The ADC to General Terence was Captain Tim Porter of the Royal Welch Fusiliers. I introduced him to my sister, and they were married on 19th December 1970 in the Chapel of RMAS followed by a reception in the India Army Room. A wonderful wedding in every respect. One of the highlights for me was that of my magisterial Aunt Jean. She had two attractive 18 year old twin daughters on her hands. Mid reception, presumably on sighting a potential son in law, she was heard to command "Twins follow me"!

I should mention that we had been allocated an army Quarter in Bulford, number 5 Gaza Road, Bulford. It was probably the coldest house the army possessed. It has since been demolished!

The author's wife, Mona

It was at this time that I decided we must have a home of our own. We had been in seventeen houses in twelve years of marriage! We were lucky enough to find and buy a charming small cottage in 1969, in Penton Mewsey, near Andover. This was ideal for a small commute to Bulford and the possibility of a weekly commute to Latimer. The girls loved Penton Mewsey, a very friendly village with school in walking distance. We acquired the first family dog (a puppy!), a beautiful Red Setter that was to be called Lisa. She was highly strung and a bit potty, but Jane just adored her. When they had both been naughty, one would find Jane and Lisa curled up in the same dog basket! It is funny that Jackie was quite circumspect about this first animal in the house. She was later to adore her own dogs.

Latimer loomed. I heard that I had been selected to attend the one year first course of the newly established National Defence Collage (NDC) at Latimer. The Commandant was to be General Terence McMeekin!

NDC was great fun. Ten students from each Service and a sprinkling of overseas students. I believe the aim was to widen the political grasp of the conduct of world affairs. Most guest speakers were excellent and debate at many levels, stimulating.

From Latimer I was posted to Rheindahlen, Germany as Military Assistant (MA) to the Chief of Staff, BAOR, General David House. We were given a very pleasant, tied army quarter (tied to the appointment). I was a bit anxious on two counts. First, the General did not smoke; I gave up. Second, he was purported to have one of the sharpest brains in the army and did not suffer fools gladly. It was a stimulating job covering a vast field of military and quasi political matters. Happily, I had a good work partnership with John Learmonth, who was upstairs as MA to the CinC BAOR General Sir Peter Hunt.

I had not been an MA before, but quickly found it to be at times a humbling job or one which yielded much power. The monthly plenary meeting of Staff taken by General David was a case in point. The ground floor of the main building where we worked was like a maze. The room for plenary meetings was a good three minutes' walk door to door and I did at least three, if not four, reconnaissance trips of the route and was terrified of losing the General en route. I just knew that he did not know the route and was happy to follow me! Having jumped that hurdle, it was my job to take verbatim notes of every item under discussion. Probably 20 participants. The following day I had to publish, on behalf of the Chief of Staff, the Minutes of the meeting. Not surprisingly, the General vetted them before release.

On the power side, nobody could have an appointment with the Chief of Staff without going through me and also my office. Tact was important, especially when dealing with busy Brigadiers.

On a good morning, around midday out would come the sherry. He did not like the previous Military Assistant's (MA) choice of glasses, the lack of a decanter, and a metal tray. Cut glass decanter and sherry glasses with a silver tray were in his office by the next morning!

It was about this time that schooling for younger daughter, Jane, reared its head. We decided she should join her sister, Jackie, at Tildonk Convent, Louvain, where, funnily enough, General David's daughter had been. Whilst Jackie put up with it, Jane did not follow suit. In the event we have been blessed with two spirited and wonderful daughters.

We left Germany in 1973 after one year in the job. General David House was to become GOC Northern Ireland.

I was to take over as Commanding Officer of the 1st Battalion The Royal Scots at Tidworth on 1st December 1973. It turned out the next 2½ years were extremely active.

My dormant love for France was probably stirred up by holiday visits. Also, by an enticing press campaign in the early 70s to persuade people that France was a land of milk and honey cluttered with quaint houses that cost little.

I was on leave at the time in Penton Mewsey preparing for a year's weekly commute for the first course at NDC Latimer. I grasped the French nettle and booked a flight to Paris!

Some days later I got off a French train at Périgueux in South West France. I walked half a mile into town with a small case. I knew no one, had no agent or contacts. I popped into a nearby 'Tabac' for a glass of wine and a sandwich hoping to find someone who might recommend somewhere to stay. "Bonsoir, je m'appelle Raymond, vous etes anglais?" said the person sat next to me at the bar.

It so happened that Raymond and his wife who lived in Oxfordshire were on a short holiday in Périgueux. He was a teacher by profession but as a side-line dealt in the French property market for English buyers! He fixed up my accommodation. We met for breakfast in the morning and then set off to find that elusive but enchanting French property. After several false starts we spotted through the mist a square white farmhouse on a hilltop above Montignac. We drove up a long track on which, halfway up there was a working farm. We finally reached our objective, an abandoned farmhouse with an orchard and possibly land.

Had we cracked it? A dream come true? Raymond introduced me to an 'Immobilier' in Périgueux who said the owner was a farmer now retired to Lyons, the other side of France. The farmer would possibly be anxious to sell.

I returned to Penton Mewsey in a couple of days quite excited. I have to say, Mona did not share this excitement.

In fact, we went off on the new posting to Rheindahlen, Germany, the headquarters of the British Army of the Rhine (BAOR). Our two girls, Jackie and Jane were now at the convent school in Louvain, Belgium, Thus as a family we were all about to be Europe-based: a further incentive for seeking a French property. We settled into Rheindahlen, and it was not too long before I persuaded Mona that we should motor from Germany across France to the Dordogne. A very scenic drive, especially through the Jura region. One of the nicest wines I have ever tasted, a Jura Pinot Noir.

We arrived at Périgueux and with the French agent alongside, went to see the house on the hill near Montignac. The farmer halfway up the hill, occupying the only other property, was not too keen to acknowledge us. He was using the twelve hectares of land belonging to the property we were hoping to buy.

Finally, after much haggling, humming, and harring, we did a deal. We then motored back to Rheindahlen. At the first opportunity, we returned to France with the girls for our first stay at La Bonne Lie. We were suitably armed with camping gear. Inside, the house was burdened with wet and dry rot, but one could see the potential through shape and size. It was waterproof and apart from windows and shutters that we had fixed there were no big problems. The girls had to bathe in the huge wooden wine vat that was in the delightful, cobbled courtyard. Much fun was had in the setting evening sun with hosepipe in one hand and a glass of wine in the other. There was a 'privé rustique' in the orchard. I could sit there for hours breathing in the scent from the herbs and flowers which bees were busy pollinating; beware the odd French hornet too!

The neighbouring French farmer and his family became more friendly. We agreed he could continue to work our land in exchange for fresh milk and eggs as well as logs when needed. We were invited several times down to his farmhouse. We would all sit in the kitchen round a table drinking Alsace wine. Grandma would be sitting comfortably in an armchair with a seemingly contented goose on her lap. The goose seemed to be totally relaxed as corn was fed down its throat using a small funnel.

We really enjoyed frequent trips down to the Dordogne during the summer. Of course. in the early seventies it was yet to be overcrowded with the English. Sadly, this adventure with a house in Gascony for the family came to an abrupt end. I had been at Rheindahlen for exactly a year when I heard I was to command the regiment from 1st December 1973. This involved a move to Tidworth and subsequent duties in Norway, Cyprus, Scotland, and Northern Ireland!

We kept the house near Montignac on for the next summer. We did not let it but our girls allowed some of their young friends to use

The author's elder daughter, Jacqueline

it for holidays. They were punctilious with thank you letters. A small parcel arrived for my wife one day with an accompanying letter from a young friend. It contained the following passage:

I MET A MOUSE.
HE WAS A FRENCH MOUSE.
HE TAUGHT ME TO SPEAK FRENCH, AND I TAUGHT HIM SOME ENGLISH.
THE POT OF JAM ENCLOSED WAS MADE BY MONSIEUR MOUSE FROM FRUIT IN YOUR ORCHARD.

We later sold this, our first house in France. We were not to return for thirty years. Having waited those thirty years, we did make a pilgrimage from our next French house back to La Bonne Lit. On arrival we saw two senior ladies on their knees – weeding. Wonderful, it was the same two sisters from Paris who had bought our first French property all those years ago.

15

Cyprus 1974

The 30th of November was St Andrew's Day, the end of which was always celebrated by a Guest Night in the Officers' Mess. It so happens that I had met Mona, my wife to be, at a St Andrew's Day ball in the Mess in the Canal Zone of Egypt in 1954.

I kept well away from Assaye Barracks, Tidworth on the 30th November 1973 ready to take command the next day. We spent the night locally with friends. At about 1am, the 'phone rings. It was the duty officer from the battalion reporting that the Ministry of Defence had put us on 24-hour Notice to deploy to Northern Ireland. It occurred to me that the Officers were unlikely to have clear heads before 10am. I sent a message back by 'phone. 1000 hours CO Order Group (OGp). Before 10am we moved down to 10 days' Notice to move. The Jocks responded as ever with much enthusiasm, although I detected a slight worry from some wives. We had previously been advised the battalion's next tour was to be two years in Cyprus accompanied by families. This had been planned as a reward for the considerable strain on soldiers and families in the ACE Mobile Force (Land) (AMF(L)) which involved winter deployments to Norway and summer exercises in Greece or Turkey or both. The role of AMF(L) was further interspersed with Emergency tours of four months' duration in Northern Ireland.

In the event, having been stood down in December 1973 for Northern Ireland, I was able to take a tactical HQ and two companies to Norway in late winter 1973. Langlaufing on skis was new to me and I was quickly under the tutelage of one of our very able and charming Norwegian military ski instructors. We had some fairly rough and tough exercises in weather about 40° below.

I think I fell eyes wide open to one little test. The Belgian two-star commander of AMF(L) who was running an exercise sent for me one morning and said: "meet me at "place X" on the map this afternoon at 1500 hours to discuss a further plan.". Robert Watson, my Operations Officer at the time, studied the map carefully with me. We identified a tiny mark at a particularly high point in the mountain ranges. We could only go so far by helicopter because of fuel shortages. We disembarked on a considerable high slope, nothing but virgin snow. Robert excelled "come on Colonel, this way" he said. On and on we went and were fairly pooped. I was physically a touch soft after the corridors of HQ BAOR.

We finally made it with about five minutes to spare. The General greeted us with a wry smile: "just a little examination" he said. "I'll give you a lift back in my helicopter just parked out of sight".

Another experience was the conduct of arctic trials which the MoD was very keen for us to do. This particular trial was to test the multi-role efficacy of some white candles. We were to dig a small snowhole for three in which to spend the night. No lighting, no heating, no food, but some air.

The aim of the trial was that the candles would produce light, provide heat, and if necessary, food. They would, of course, extinguish if there was no air. Not surprisingly, we completed the MoD trial report, and our recommendations were pretty negative to put it politely!

We departed Norway, after four winters in the role, by ship from Bergen. The previous evening, we hosted a party in Bergen Castle for our many Norwegian friends.

Whilst we were in Norway completing our last tours in the AMF(L) role, much work was bring done in Tidworth in preparation for the forthcoming accompanied 2-year tour in Cyprus. With some help from staff in Cyprus, we obtained quite a lot of information about living conditions for families, shopping in Limassol, and many photographs of the army hirings that families would occupy in Limassol. All this detail was passed on at Tidworth at various Wives' Club meetings.

In May 1974, we deployed to Cyprus as the sole resident battalion, accompanied by families, numbering some 250 women and children. Spirits were high on arrival in the Mediterranean sunshine. All ranks got stuck into becoming fully conversant with the internal security role before settling down to enjoying the potential delights of a sunshine tour! It was not to be!

In July 1974, Turkish mainland forces, spearheaded by an airborne drop, invaded northern Cyprus. They made rapid progress to the outskirts of Nicosia and towards Famagusta. I recall being rung at home at 3am on invasion morning by a staff officer of HQ Land Forces Cyprus and being asked did I know about it and what was I going to do?!

It was at this time that the Foreign Secretary, Jim Callaghan was en-route by air to Africa for meetings. On hearing the news about Cyprus, the aircraft was immediately diverted, and conversations followed with Air Marshal Aitken, Commander British Forces Cyprus (CBFC) and Major General Hugh Butler, Commander Land Forces Cyprus (CLFC).

That evening, CBFC gives a Dinner Party for Jim Callaghan to which many of the great and the good were invited including John Wilberforce, the High Commissioner from Nicosia. I was lucky enough, as Commanding Officer of the only battalion in the Western Sovereign Base Area (WSBA) to be included.

After dinner, CBFC invited Mr Callaghan, his PPS, the High Commissioner, and one or two others including me to his study for discussion. I tucked myself into a corner and listened avidly to the discussions about how to react to the Turkish landings bearing in mind Turkey was a NATO ally, and the UK Government a joint guarantor of the security of the Island. After much to-ing and fro-ing, somebody said "I think we should ask Henry". Who on earth was Henry? I thought.

The Foreign Secretary turned to his PPS saying, "get a flash telegram off to Henry now explaining our predicament and asking for his counsel".

It was not long before advice came back from Henry Kissinger on the lines "no intervention, protect your facilities, NATO to discuss".

The battalion rapidly deployed to secure the perimeter boundaries of the WSBA to protect key points, to establish permanent roadblocks, to keep open the main supply route between the Sovereign Base and the airhead and the temporary dock facility at RAF Akrotiri. This latter task was accomplished with much energy and elan by the Recce P1 led by Lt Johnstone. They were in between firefights between local Greek and Turkish Cypriots.

It was at this time there was a mini crisis at the front gates to RAF Akrotiri. The defence or entry to the gates and of about 20 metres of tarmac road leading to them was entirely the responsibility of the Akrotiri-based RAF Regiment squadron. Some Cypriot hooligans saw this as a weak spot and tipped over two or three heavy RAF vehicles and an RAF car in which SASO was exiting the base. Johnstone was alerted to this and with one Land Rover and six Jocks drove off the yobs in quick time. The problem was not repeated.

In addition to deployments and many other jobs to be done in the WSBA, we were invited to protect all the officers and senior NCOs houses with a barbed wire enclosure. This was a huge job made more difficult by the cliff-side incline on which the quarters were built. The Jocks endeared themselves to the families with sheer hard work with razor wire in extreme heat. Fortunately, cold drinks, tea, and grapes flowed out of the houses. Our Scottish soldiers made their names for their consideration and politeness.

All this frenetic activity had its lighter moments. The Brigadier Scottish Division, Brig Tony Findlay, chose to arrive for a week's visit to the battalion the day the Turks invaded and the adjutant, Captain Mark Strudwick, had to use all his diplomatic skills to get the Brigadier out of my hair and out of Cyprus! The Signals Officer, Captain Finlay McLean, assisted our smooth, but overworked communications by being caught while on leave with his wife behind Turkish lines in northern Cyprus! They bravely made it back within 36 hours after a hazardous trip.

As the situation developed and became more threatening, I was invited by HQ Land Forces to implement the planned evacuation from Limassol of all service families including the majority of our families. Needless to say, the plan did not take account of serious firefights between local Greek and Turkish Cypriots with our families in the middle!

To assist in the extraction of families, I instructed Lt Simon Barnetson to accompany the District Officer, Fayik Muftizade, (well known to me in Cyprus 55), on a mission to establish a temporary truce with the warring Cypriots in Limassol. This small party, Land Rover borne and flying a huge Union Jack, were fired at, stopped by gunmen, and disarmed. After a very tense standoff, they were allowed to enter Limassol. With some difficulty, the party achieved a truce, and the evacuation then began under the auspices of the Families Officer, Major Ian MacLachlan. Barnetson was subsequently awarded the Queen's Gallantry Medal for his action.

The Service families were led out of Limassol. They were much uplifted on arrival at the Sovereign Base boundary by the sight and sound of Piper Cornwall. Allocation of temporary accommodation was a nightmare. My wife, amongst others, put up 47 evacuees on night one, thereafter 17 over a 10-day period. The lot in our 3-bedroom Quarter and garden.

Rations and feeding these numbers were not without difficulty. Mona had a team of very helpful wives around her. There were army rations delivered daily, but they were 'compo' tinned and dessicated field rations. They were not taken up as being wholly unsuitable for the many young. Instead, our freezer was raided, and much pork, chicken, and lamb enjoyed by all. At the time, I was sleeping in the Operations Room and used to pop home for half an hour just after midnight. There I would come across some good parties being held by the wives after coping with the young all day. The drink cupboard was looking bare too!

A lull ensued and the families returned to Limassol. HQ 19 Airportable Brigade assumed command and a Commando unit arrived as reinforcement.

At the same time, events outside the compass of the battalion were building up. A considerable fleet of RN ships was off the coast and had accomplished tricky evacuations of other British and Foreign nationals. Fighter and bomber aircraft had flown into RAF Akrotiri.

The station was commanded by Air Commodore Don Hall, who had flown just about every aircraft that existed. He and his wife were charming to Mona and me. On the operational side, he could not have been more helpful, and his door was always open.

Trouble brewed again, and a second evacuation of families was ordered by CBFC. A punitive force was stood up, comprising A Company, led by Major Edward Cowan with a half Squadron of

The Blues and Royals under command. This force was positioned within a few miles of Limassol ready to intervene should the evacuation run into serious difficulties. In the event, the extraction of families went smoothly but CBFC directed that families should now be repatriated direct back to the UK. Our families, with only one suitcase each, were given a send-off in the middle of the night by the Regimental Military Band. Goodbyes were very sparse because of operational commitments. The disparate arrival of families in Scotland was handled very energetically and with much sympathy by Regimental HQ.

Farwell Parade for General Campbell, Cyprus 1974

Meanwhile, C Company, led by Major Mike Ashmore, had to conduct a very sensitive evacuation of Turkish Cypriots who were being threatened in their village, close to the Sovereign Base, by EOKA 'B' gunmen. The successful rescue operation resulted in our having to establish a large temporary refugees' camp within the Base for Turkish Cypriot families who were under threat.

There swiftly followed a threat to the RAF radar domes in the Troodos Mountains. 42 Commando was an obvious choice to deal with the situation as we were so committed. However, Brigadier Glover, commander 19 Brigade, agreed that the Pipes and Drums mount a heliborne assault. A stirring and unique moment as the Pipes and Drums deployed, fully bombed up, under the leadership of the Drum Major. Their threatening arrival in Wessex helicopters on the mountain top put paid to any further nonsense.

Another comparative lull in events occurred in the early autumn of 1974 by which time the battalion was settled into a 10-month unaccompanied tour! Further respite was ensured by my CASEVAC to UK with back trouble. Majors Ashmore and Cowan took the opportunity to stage a big production in Happy Valley of the 'Battle of Culloden'. Even the Chief of the General Staff, General Sir Peter Hunt, an attendant highlander, was impressed!

I returned to duty in November and took back the reigns from the acting CO, Lt Col Stuart McBain. Thereafter the battalion became largely responsible for sweeping up Turkish Cypriots for evacuation to the North of the Island via RAF Akrotiri and onward flight to Turkey. At about this time too, the ESBA was reinforced by a battalion of 10GR. We took full advantage of swapping Jocks for Gurkhas, which all seemed to enjoy.

All ranks of The Royal Scots left Cyprus in February 1975 for Scotland with heads held high and the gratitude of many on the Island.

Briefing Major General Hugh Butler, Commander Land Forces Cyprus (CLFC) during the Turkish invasion troubles

16
Northern Ireland

The Battalion was based at Kirknewton Camp, Edinburgh in March 1975 following the tour in Cyprus. Families were reunited and a well-earned leave ensued.

Minds were set on the prospect of a four-month tour in South Armagh in the autumn. 'The best laid plans .....!'. Leave was interrupted by a telephone call from the MOD to take the battalion to Glasgow and clean the dustbins! A first for the Regiment, but nobody was amused, least of all three Company Commanders who were to have the privilege of camping at Glasgow's three incinerator sites! Not surprisingly, the Jocks rose to the challenge and were far more efficient and sober that the Glasgow binmen. The strike was broken within weeks. I should add that in a later phone call from the MOD I was offered a pay increment of £0.08p – £0.10p a day for all ranks as an allowance for special duties. I turned it down instantly on the phone. An insult to my soldiers.

Before we left Glasgow, the Lord Provost's Office contacted my team and asked if I would agree to parade the Companies concerned so that the city could give its thanks formally. Of course, we agreed, we paraded on a wet and windy Glasgow day and the Lord Provost made a generous speech of thanks. The matter of Glasgow's dustbins was rounded off by the presentation to every soldier participant of a mug and a miniature bottle of whisky!!

Training for Northern Ireland began in April and followed the usual pattern with two exceptions. First, every Company was split into four-man teams which had to be rigidly stuck to, and second, the battalion 2ic, Major Francis Gibb, worked up an excellent innovative exercise for the culmination of our training in Norfolk. The Stanford Training Area was transformed into a replica of Southern Armagh, which included no movement other than by helicopter, to and between the replicated bases at Forkhill, Bessbrook, and Crossmaglen. All likely rural incidents were meticulously rehearsed. It was quickly proven by A Company who were involved in a serious incident near to Crossmaglen within minutes of assuming operational responsibility.

The battalion had, by this time, completed many successful tours in Northern Ireland, but this was the first in the infamous so-called 'Bandit Country'. It is important to stress that this four-month tour was much in the hands of our young soldiers, the L/Corporals and Corporals who led the four-man bricks constantly under pressure. They excelled!

Prior to the battalion's arrival in South Armagh, the IRA gunmen tended to stand off south of the border which led to inconsequential firefights. The IRA also appeared to dominate the Dublin-Belfast railway in the border area and tried to hijack trains at will and disable them. To counter this scenario, I directed that within the border area we should attempt to lure the gunmen into our area of responsibility. Simultaneously, the Secretary of State, Mervyn Rees, personally directed, through Commander Land Forces, Major General David Young, that there were to be no more train hijackings!

A Company, led by Major Edward Cowan, had the task of dominating the area around Crossmaglen with a view to ambushing IRA gunmen. They operated an extensive and aggressive patrol programme by day and night. As a result of a particular ambush operation, Private Buchanan was awarded the Military Medal.

In terms of domination, A Company set the pattern on the first night of operations by ringing the town of Crossmaglen with steel. This allowed me to visit and enter every one of some dozen public houses in the town square – the message was simply to announce that The Royal Scots had arrived!

B Company, led by Major Bob Patterson, had a similar task at Forkhill. The Company's first priority, however, was to stop the train hijackings in the border area. This B Company did with great success and there was no further hijack during the rest of the tour.

C Company, led by Major Mike Ashmore, had a very busy urban role in support of the RUC in Newry. At the time, Newry was a hotbed of Republican activity. During one of many vehicle check point operations, the Company uncovered the biggest find to date of high explosive mix and detonators, all concealed within a large petrol tanker.

Sp Company, led by Major Ron Brotherton, operated in support of the RUC out of Newton Hamilton. This was a notorious area for spasmodic IRA activity. The Company dominated the area by foot and Land Rover patrols. It was in the night that a mobile patrol was blown up by a remote wire controlled explosive device. There resulted the tragic loss of three young Royal Scots soldiers, Privates Bannon, Pearson, and Ferguson.

Battalion HQ and HQ Company were based at Bessbrook Mill. It was from Bessbrook that the battalion ran the biggest helicopter operating base in the Province. The highly professional support that we received from RN, Army and RAF pilots was second to none. They operated by day and night in all weather and made a huge contribution.

The battalion was privileged to be asked, through Commander 3 Infantry Brigade, Brigadier David Anderson, to field the first detachment of SAS to be deployed in Ulster. The Director SAS,

Brigadier Johnny Watts, briefed me and familiarisation training was arranged with A Company at Crossmaglen and with the Recce P1 led by Lt Jim Blythe. He will recall the covetous eyes of the SAS on the specialist equipment held by Recce P1 which the SAS did not have!

Throughout the tour, we had enormous and unfettered support from higher formations, the RUC and various other agencies. Michael McAtameny, Divisional RUC Commander and 'H' Jones, BM of 3 Brigade, were especially close and helpful to the battalion. Surpassing all however, was the indomitable spirit of our soldiers who never faltered under very trying living and operating conditions.

The tour ended in February 1976. The esteem in which the battalion was held in the Province was marked by an unprecedented farewell escort of RAF helicopters of our ship from Belfast Dock well into the Irish Sea. We returned to Kirknewton for leave followed by a change in command.

Bessbrook Mill

661 SQUADRON ARMY AIR CORPS
BRITISH FORCES POST OFFICE 41

his is to certify that on 6th April 1976

Lt-Col P M Davies OBE

Commanding Officer of 1st Batallion the Royal Scots

achieved a total of

100 hours

in his privately owned chauffeur driven Army Department helicopter

T. N. Taylor

Officer Commanding
661 Squadron
Army Air Corps

17

Staff College – Two

Just before we finished in Northern Ireland and I handed over command to Lt Col Stuart McBain, I was informed of my next posting. After a spot of gardening leave, I was to go to the Staff College, Camberley as a member of the Directing Staff (DS).

I was to start in the autumn of 1976. Straightaway it was evident that not a lot had changed since I was a student there 13 years earlier. It has now totally changed and has moved to Shrivenham! The DS were officers selected prior to command of their regiment or unit. In addition, a few old laggards who had just 'commanded' were selected as DS. I was one of them! In fact, from my own experience I have little doubt that the post command DS can generate a touch more confidence with student officers.

I was in the Basic Tactics team. Not quite so basic as the nomenclature suggests. The team were responsible for the setting and writing of tactical exercises up to Divisional level. Days were generally divided up with syndicate work indoors, outdoor activity, and perhaps a DS presentation in the theatre. In order to keep up, a fair amount of work in the evenings was required of students. It was just my luck that almost the day I appeared the command structure of units at Brigade level in BAOR changed. This of course meant every tactical paper for writing or discussion by students had to be re-written by the DS. No more retrieving by DS to pull out a good exercise from the files of ten or even one year ago! I found myself up at 4am many mornings trying to keep up. Contrary to some opinion being a DS at Camberley in the late 70s was no sinecure.

1976 was a real low in terms of Pay and Conditions of Service for the Armed Forces. It was a subject causing much discussion and anger amongst the Staff College student body. At the height of this serious discontent, it was timely that Denis Healey MP, then Chancellor of the Exchequer was due to address the students and Directing Staff. The Commandant of the Staff College, General John Stanier, was clearly aware of the depth of feelings on army pay. In an unprecedented address to all in the Alanbrooke Hall, before the appearance of Mr Healey, the Commandant said words to the effect "I am aware of certain matters, and I know that you will all give the Chancellor a warm welcome and listen with courtesy to what he has to say". Of course, that is exactly the response Mr Healey received.

The concern about Pay and Conditions of Service has never evaporated and is probably the 'raison d'etre' behind poor recruitment and retention throughout the Armed Services.

There were two real highlights to the year at Camberley. The Pantomime which had a really high local reputation and of course was a hot house for army actors! The real plum in my view was the Battlefield Tour in the summer. It was an on- the-spot retelling of operations in Normandy, France following D-Day.

In 1977, the tour was devised and produced by a member of the DS, the late Major General Sir Michael Hobbs. He was the team leader, and we were all transported by the realism and effort he put into recreating the scene. To describe events as they actually happened, he had mustered between the beaches and Bocage of Normandy: commanders who seized vital bridges over the Caen canal and River Orne, commanders of armoured units who had heavy losses on the approach to Bourguébus ridge; Hans von Luck whose 88mm anti-aircraft unit inflicted heavy losses against British tanks in a direct fire mode. And many others too – we learned of the VC won by the legendary Company Sergeant Major Hollis of the Green Howards storming a German bunker.

I have read much about the Normandy landings but that is nothing compared to listening to the warriors of yesterday on both sides of the conflict.

In the autumn of 1977, I was told at Camberley that I was to command 19 Airportable Brigade from January 1978.

18

19 Airportable Brigade

The headquarters of the brigade was at Colchester in Goojerat Barracks. My family were provided with an excellent army Quarter, Friday Wood Lodge, situated in the countryside.

I duly took over from Brigadier Richard Vincent who was later to become Field Marshal! Dick had warned me by phone at Camberley that one of my first tasks as the new Brigade Commander would be to do a 'presentation' for the Commander in Chief, UK Land Forces at Wilton. The subject was to be: How training could be improved at brigade level in BAOR.

The date for the presentation in front of a row of 2-star Generals from BAOR was mind-blowing. It was now January, and the presentation was to take place towards the end of March. My experience of soldiering in Germany was almost nil. A few days in Osnabrück before being banished to the Libyan desert and one year behind a desk as MA to the Chief of Staff BAOR!

Sadly, the presentation did not go as well as I had hoped. I had misjudged the priorities in my own Brigade HQ. Preparation for the presentation should have had absolute priority over other pressing business.

I suspect the Commander in Chief, General Dwyn Bramall, was less than happy, which of course is not a great stimulant for a career soldier!

Whilst this little drama was going on, we were within moments of converting from a brigade force into a Field Force. The principal change was the addition of a number of Territorial Army major and minor units. Numerically we were then doubled in size to about 13,000 strong.

The formation of the new unit involved much detailed staff work shared between Major David Lowe and Major Malcolm Grant-Howarth, my two principal staff officers. We were all out of the same egg – Staff College 1976 – a triple yolk of one DS and two graduates.

The main role of the new Field Force was to have the ability to move swiftly to northern Germany in support of any of the British Divisions. Such moves had to be practised many times. Planning for the amount of artillery, armour, engineers and the poor bloody infantry was complex and involved shipping, air, rail and road movement. We were always given great support by HQ Eastern District commanded by Major General Andy Watson.

I recall another minor difficulty with a different CinC from Wilton. He was visiting Colchester and 7 Field Force at Goojerat Barracks for the first time. I laid on a briefing and kicked off. "Before you go any further Philip, tell me about Goojerat – why Goojerat Barracks?" he said. I replied "General, you have bowled me out first ball". He smiled; we went on!

Despite one or two little hiccoughs, I know that the team I had with me all enjoyed enormously the challenging work we faced. Of course, we took the view there was no better trained or more flexible force in the Army. It was later in the year that I heard I was to spend 1980 as a member of The Royal College of Defence Studies (RCDS) in Belgravia.

The family moved back to our little cottage in Penton Mewsey. Elder daughter Jackie was doing well working in London, and younger daughter Jane was doing some cooking jobs in London, in ski lodges, and on boats. To cap it all, during the year we bought another house and moved to Upton Lovell, Wiltshire. The lure of fishing on a strip of the River Wylye running through the garden was unstoppable!

19

RCDS

The year at RCDS started in January 1980. The first problem was whether to participate with my wife in the year or should I be a weekly commuter once more. An easy decision really because Mona by now, in 24 years of marriage, had tackled 25 houses. So, the family decamped to Upton Lovell, and I found an agreeable weekly lodging in London near Belgrave Square.

The aim of the course was to broaden the minds of those expected to progress up the ladder. Emphasis was on political, foreign, civil, and military affairs. The split of graduates was roughly ten from each of the Armed Services, ten from a blend of Foreign Office, Civil Service and Police Service. In addition, a very welcome mix of ten from Worldwide countries.

Syndicates often were the forum for discussion and debate on a huge range of topics. The DS were a team of high-priced civil servants and military staff. The whole under the leadership of Air Chief Marshal Sir Robert Freer.

I must confess that never in my 30 years' service had I been in more congenial surroundings than those at number 37 Belgrave Square. An elegant period property fitted out most carefully to provide syndicate rooms, library, restaurant, and bar. The whole conducive to a very relaxed atmosphere which permeated our days not least with overseas colleagues.

The highlight of the year was the Overseas Tour. The world was divided into regions: USA, Far East, Middle East, and Europe. One was given a choice of which region you would like to visit over a period of about three weeks, I chose the USA.

I had never been to America and in 1980 our team tour included Canada, USA and Mexico City. It is worth mentioning we were not just tourists having a caper. The programme was fulfilled at a high level and we were to meet with folk of considerable authority.

We landed in Quebec on an Autumn day to be met by a French-Canadian guard of honour. Then escorted to a lavish luncheon laid on by the French-Canadian armed forces. All speeches were conducted in French as was the fluent reply given by our team leader, Major General Roy Redgrave. Then onwards to Ottawa, Toronto, through the Rockies by special train ending up in British Columbia, then by sea plane to Vancouver Island and a welcome from Canadian Scottish pipers!

I think we then arrived in New York pretty frazzled, and we had only just begun!

Our main engagement was a luncheon given for us by the United Nations Secretariat at the top of the World Trade Centre (a target of the 9/11 terrorist attack).

We then were whisked off to Chicago, Detroit, and Los Angeles. In Detroit we had very interesting conversations with union leaders of the car industry which was about to self-immolate.

For me, some unforgettable moments were spent with the Chicago Police Department. We were to meet at 7pm (local) and go out on patrol in separate police cars. Dressed in my normal clothes as instructed. I watched as a whole load of weapons were stowed in the trunk of the police car – rifles, shotguns, gas grenades, etc. Off we set. It seemed not five minutes before the first call: "robbery at supermarket". On arrival I was told "watch but do not move, we will cover you". Not a lot happened then "a shooting on X street"; we arrived in a cloud of burning rubber. "You get out here, Sir, but don't move". The night went on with no pause in incidents. The police crew and I returned to the station at 1am after an apparent quiet night on patrol!

The visit to Mexico City was a first for all our group. We were probably a touch blasé by now with more welcoming speeches and lunches. I was stunned by the overcrowding in the city – you could hardly move. I took the opportunity to buy some gifts for Mona and the two girls. They each got a ring with a different precious stone mounted. Sadly, they have all been lost!

And so, a fascinating year came to an end. It was in November that I learned my next appointment was to be Commander Land Forces, Cyprus (CLFC). Third time lucky?

20

Cyprus 1981

Christmas 1980 was spent at home in Upton Lovell. There was much family excitement about Cyprus and the thought of living at Flagstaff House. Daughter Jackie continued to do well in her job in London, but Jane, now aged 19, was to come with us. Inevitably the question of clothes for Mum came up.

Off the two of us go to London. We park in Knightsbridge and pop into Harrods for a sandwich. Mona was keen to see what she could find in the way of summer clothes. We agree to meet up in the Green Man (internal Harrods pub) at 4pm prior to the journey home. I picked up an Evening Standard to see how I could occupy myself for the two to three hours. It just so happened that the Boat Show was on at Earls Court. I was intrigued, not least with the thought of two years of Cyprus in mind. Sure enough, about an hour later I was arranging a marine mortgage for the purchase of a Dutch-built, double hulled 26′ yacht, two berths, etc. It would be delivered to any port on the south coast for export.

Four o'clock loomed and I met up with Mona. She is looking pale and almost in tears. It turned out that she really could not find anything suitable or what she did like was a ridiculous price. I sympathised as hard as I could and then broke the news that I had bought a boat. There was a dreadful long hush!

Over the next week or two we resolved the issue with the help of daughters. The two of them were a touch more on my side –

Flagstaff House, Cyprus

Ariadne, Paphos Harbour

an enjoyable asset for two years. In the event, Mona had a successful day in London with Jackie – shopping!

How to get the boat to Cyprus? The Royal Navy came to the rescue. For a small charge of £30 they would ship it out 'on deck' on a frigate scheduled to visit the Island.

It was in January that I began to hear some gossip from Cyprus that the staff of the newly appointed Commander British Forces Cyprus (CBFC), Air Vice Marshal Len Davis were hoping to purloin the services of two elderly Sudanese servants from Flagstaff House to Air House. By signal to the Army staff, I made it clear that the two servants were indentured army servants. These games were not over. I subsequently heard that the Chief Officer of the Sovereign Base Area (COSBA), a civil servant, was hoping, due to his seniority, to move into Flagstaff House. True or not, probably apocryphal, it was nipped in the bud.

Towards the end of January, the three of us left Brize Norton for the four-hour flight to Cyprus. After about two hours it was obvious daughter Jane was in much pain. We thought a dormant tooth abscess might have swollen due to air pressure. The crew were very helpful and radioed RAF Akrotiri where the hospital was located. Jane was first off the aircraft in Cyprus and re-joined us later after some dental work.

Flagstaff was probably one of the choicest residencies worldwide available to an army commander. We were extremely fortunate. That fortune was duplicated when we met Ahwhad and Sam. These two Sudanese servants had come to Cyprus just after the war in service to the Commander Middle East Land Forces. They were gems. When taking breakfast up to a lady guest Ahwhad would ensure the rose on the tray had a drop of dew on it – from the tap!

There were and still are two principal British Sovereign Bases on the Island, RAF Akrotiri as part of the Western Sovereign Base Area (WSBA) and the Eastern Sovereign Base Area (ESBA) at Dhekelia.

The continuing existence of the bases was ratified by the Treaty of Guarantee 1960 between UK, Cyprus, Greece, and Turkey.

The role of British forces was quite simply to maintain the security of the SBAs and all living and working in the bases. There were also good facilities for training. A wild peninsula named Akamas was particularly suitable for visiting unit exercises such as RMAS and the SAS. There were two major units: one battalion in the WSBA normally on a two-year tour – odes of Cyprus 1974! and the other battalion rotated every six months through the ESBA with 50% rebadged as UN and patrolling the divide in Nicosia between Cyprus and the so- called Turkish/Cypriot north. The ESBA at Dhekelia was close to Larnaca where, at the time the main Cypriot airport was situated. Aya Napa on the far side of the ESBA was a favourite beach front for the young worldwide.

The garrison at Dhekelia was commanded by Douglas McCord, an old friend of mine from the Ulster Rifles. He and his wife led a very busy life which included entertaining visiting firemen. To take some of the strain we sent him Sam, one of our two Sudanese servants; help that was much appreciated. I recall a moment when the strain in the ESBA was a touch tense; I went down to see Douglas. We went to the ESBA Sailing Club, climbed into a Mirror dinghy, and spent the morning doing man overboard drills. Good and refreshed in all departments!

Not too onerous a military task, Cyprus was there to be enjoyed. A rare moment for the servicemen and women, and perhaps their families, to enjoy beaches and the sun throughout the year. I tried to talk to every new young officer arriving on the Island: "master your job and then enjoy life in Cyprus".

Our daughter, Jane, took the opportunity to enjoy life quite seriously. She first went off to do a stint in an Israeli kibbutz. This, although admirable, did not get off to a good start. At Larnaca airport, checking in for Tel Aviv, she was held up. What are you doing – born in Benghazi, Libya?!! We don't know, but there may have been Israeli agents involved. She then loses her wallet and money! Fortunately, I was in contact with an Israeli General who had been a colleague on the RCDS year in 1980.

She climbed Mount Masada where Jews committed mass suicide under harsh Roman rule, then sets off for Eilat, trekking across Sinai. Fortunately, she is picked up and given a lift by a truck driver. On arrival in Eilat, she stays in a cave by the sea as the only hotelier seems likely to wish to accost her.

Most of this hazardous adventure was unknown to us at the time. Mona is in hospital at RAF Akrotiri with a broken elbow. Jane returns, walks past her mother, then a great reunion! The adventures go on for Jane, cooking on a boat, then a chalet girl for skiing in the Dolomites. I recall a rare moment when she was at Flagstaff House with us. We had the Commander in Chief UK Land Forces staying for a week. There was only one RAF flight a week for visitors.

General Sir Frank Kitson was, of his own admission, not the easiest person to get on with. Mona's legs were shaking when he arrived in the garden by helicopter. Jane, who had not appeared until breakfast the following morning, dashes down the stairs, no shoes, my jungle green trousers, hair in the biggest afro ever, "You can't have breakfast like that", says mum. "Oh mum, don't be silly". She sits next to the CinC, introduces herself and has him eating out of her hand in no time!

There were wonderful opportunities for sport in Cyprus. Cricket, soccer, athletics, at the time golf was not amongst them due to freshwater shortages. My wife and I took full advantage of our boat which had been safely delivered by the RN to a quayside at Akrotiri. Most weekends we would sail in Ariadne from the WBSA to Coral Bay west of Paphos or to Lara Bay where turtles nested. We would join up with friends who also had bought a variety of craft which included a beautiful wooden yacht rescued at Colchester from the mud at Mersea Island and lovingly restored by Anthony Collis in the UK and Cyprus. There were also two fairly ancient Turkish Cypriot motor vessels one of which the Jameson's passed on to their successors, the Woolley's. Occasionally, subject to our state and that of the sea, we would venture northwest past Akamas Point to Latchi. Possibly three boats, two under sail, my Ariadne, Anthony's wooden sailboat, and Mel Jameson or latterly John Woolley driving Merry Widdow (yes, it did have two ds!). Mona came to love Ariadne!

Latchi was a delightful little Cypriot fishing harbour not too frequented by tourists. The Chef du Port was undoubtedly Yangos, who owned and ran the principal restaurant. He was the most charming and generous rogue! He and some of his mates in the village made money by fishing for Swordfish in the Mediterranean using lines seven miles long with hooks. We had many a good extended lunch party enabled by Cypriot Brandy Sours, wine and Cypriot brandy.

Mona loved our visits there and had a way with Yangos! We were invited to his daughter's wedding which was to last three days. No present for the bride, but the more Cypriot pound notes you could slap on her whilst dancing, the better.

A few years ago, Jackie and Jane gave us a wonderful villa holiday in Cyprus. We went to Latchi and sadly found that Yangos had passed away, but we had a long chat with his widow and daughter, who were still running the restaurant.

One of the more testing activities that we restarted was the Land Forces HQ Climb across country and up Troodos Mountain. It was compulsory and every officer, NCO and clerk had to take part. A two-day climb with a pit-stop at night in the middle of nowhere! Our garrison headquarters were to provide a tented camp half-way up the climb with washing facilities, a marquee for an Officers'

Mess dinner, and breakfast for all in the morning. A considerable undertaking and brilliantly executed by Colonel Ben Cardozo, the garrison Commander.

Life outside of the SBAs was as friendly as ever with the Cypriot community. Lengthy morning cups of black coffee in the villages taken by elderly men had not changed. There was missing, however, that harmony and banter that previously existed between Greek and Turkish Cypriots. The latter had all been evacuated by the RAF to Turkey and many had found their way to Northern Cyprus.

The Greek Cypriot restaurants flourished as ever. I have yet to find anywhere else in the world that can serve up such big, juicy, and luscious barbecued pork chops. Accompanied by ever improving Cypriot wine, or perhaps a bottle of local brandy at £1C a go!

A truly wonderful two years which Jane also enjoyed. She celebrated her 21st birthday at Flagstaff. Dinner for quite a few in the garden. The party was led off by the Band of The Argyll and Sutherland Highlanders playing 'The Three-Legged Jock'. Late in the night there were reels with the help of an Argyll piper.

Our farewell to Cyprus for the third time was pretty emotional. We went by car, driven by Sgt Relph, to RAF Akrotiri, checked-in at the so-called VIP entrance and went to sit in the waiting room. We could hardly get in; it was packed with my staff and many other friends too!

Peter Foreshaw, my senior staff officer at the time, led Mona and I across the tarmac to the aircraft. We were halfway there and suddenly the Pipes and Drums of the Argylls were there to play us out. What a moment, and close to tears.

It was late in 1981 that I learned I was to be promoted to two stars on posting. Not long afterwards I learned the appointment was to be General Officer Commanding (GOC) North-West District.

I confess my first reaction was, is this a punishment posting in exchange for Cyprus? Not a very exciting or testing prospect lay ahead.

21
The North West

We set off, just the two of us for Preston in early 1983. This was a long way from the house at Upton Lovel which we had bought in 1980. Although Mona spent a year there I had only the odd weekend before leaving Preston. There was not much sensitivity in Army circles about moving and domestic arrangements. There was a general assumption that wives would follow, as of old, in the baggage train, and then do their stuff in support of their husband. In one respect, we were fortunate. I had asked for Andrew Standen McDougal, from the Regiment, to be my ADC. It was agreed, and from our viewpoint, was very successful, and fun. We had known Andrew's parents for years, although, if truth be known, his mother, Sally, was a touch wary of her eldest boy working with me!

For military purposes, England was carved up into Districts; these equated with the Police boundaries. My area of responsibility coincided with that of the Chief Constables of Liverpool, Manchester, Cumbria, Cheshire, Lancashire, and the Isle of Man. The military role of my District was to maintain security and assistance in support of the Police and Civil Power.

My Command comprised a Territorial Brigade based near Chester. Nearer to home a Territorial Army (TA) gunner unit, a TA Cavalry regiment and some TA minor units. The only regular army major unit was an infantry battalion situated north of Preston; its operational role under command of GOC North East District!

The TA units in my area were overseen by the Chairman Territorial Army Volunteer Reserve Association (TAVRA). At a welcoming lunch given by TAVRA in Chester there seemed a touch of sensitivity about my experience of the TA. I felt bound to let them know that I had more TA major units under command in 7 Field Force than existed in NW District.

Naturally, one was enthusiastic on arrival to see what could be done in the way of helping units and training. A busy programme of visits to units was put in hand. A more immediate approach was to order the regular army staff of my Headquarters back into uniform – they were a pretty raggedy lot in plain clothes!

During my time in the North West, some evidence was coming out of the Ministry of Defence about a UK-wide threat to key installations from Soviet Special Forces. I do not think this threat suddenly became apparent, but it was released to Commanders of Districts by the then Commander in Chief UKLF. Likely targets may have included communication centres, power installations, ports, and airfields. The news certainly created an increased sense of urgency to the provision of 'security' in support of the Police. Liaison became energised. I was fortunate to have very good relations with all six Chief Constables, not least with James Anderton in Manchester and Ken Oxford in Liverpool.

Of course, two of the joys of being in the North West were the people and the countryside. We had hitherto always sped through Lancashire and Cumbria en route to Scotland. I doubt that you could find more straightforward folk than those from Lancashire. If they didn't like you, they told you so; if you talked and worked with them, they were the salt of the earth. Local people were also very hospitable to my wife and me. Invitations to dinner awaited our arrival in Preston from people who we did not know well. We had entertained them in Cyprus – perhaps relations of someone serving there.

The beauty of the countryside in these parts is of course well known to most people. As a keen fly fisherman, I fished the Ribble and also took a rod on the River Lune; hard work to find a salmon but embraced in soporific summer scents! I was fortunate to get to know a charming businessman who came from the Manchester area. On several occasions he invited Andrew and me to fish a beat at Upper Floors on the Tweed. We were spoilt for fish – an unforgettable experience.

Life had its moments in the North West, not least in dealing with the number of visitors we had. In the autumn of 1985, we had a visit coming up from the Military Secretary (MS). He played a significant role in the careers and future of senior officers in the Army.

It was time for Mona and I to think of the future. Not surprisingly, after occupying 27 houses in thirty years of marriage she was not keen to move to yet another posting with me. She had really done her stuff and had my sympathy. For my part, I baulked at the possibility of another move – it was six years since we had bought the house at Upton Lovel near Warminster. We were yet to occupy it on a regular basis! MS came, stayed the night, and left for London. In conversation I said to him that I would be very happy to serve on but would prefer a posting in the South of England as we had our own property near Warminster. I added that if this were not possible then I would resign for family reasons. In a month or two I heard that Number 1 Board had endorsed my resignation. I was to leave the Army after 36 years of travel, excitement, adventure, and fun.

The mid-80s to the mid-90s were really devoted to family time. Mona and I were at Upton Lovell, retired. Jane, who had been cook, hostess, and First Mate on a yacht (Palau) in the Caribbean since 1984, married the Captain, Greg Geisel in Florida in 1987. Daughter Jessica was born in Salisbury, Wiltshire in August 1987. Jackie, who had a very successful career in the IT world met Owen Brenman,

The Author, The Spey

the actor, in London. They married in 1991. They lived in Dulwich and their first child, Hugo, was born in January 1993. A second boy, Oliver, was born in March 1995.

It was huge fun to have family from time to time at Upton Lovell. Wild duck came to the back door and strolled into the kitchen! Swans glided downstream with tiny cygnets astride their backs. A persistent kingfisher fished from an overhanging branch and Jessica was introduced, close up, to her first cow.

The author's granddaughter, Jessica – The salmon are running Papa

It is timely in my story to pay a huge tribute to Mona from the family. Just about once a year over thirty years as a soldiers wife, she has made a new home for the family. Always colourful and tasteful and based on rudiments of soft furnishing that we were able to stuff in a crate to be moved by ship or rail. She made many curtains, cushions and beautiful lampshades to create home whereever we might have been from the edge of the jungle in northern Malaya to above an Arab casino in Benghazi!

22

France Two

In retirement, we were lucky to have an annual trip to the Caribbean and Florida to see younger daughter, Jane, husband Greg, and granddaughter, Jessica. They lived in South Florida but sailed their handsome 60-foot catamaran out of Tortola, the British Virgin Islands.

Mona loved these trips, as did I. Much use was made of the yacht's rubber dinghy to get ashore to a bar or for a meal. We were in our seventies, and Mona undertook the leaps from boat to dinghy with much aplomb invariably landing in the arms of the Captain.

Florida – The Author and Mona on Greg's boat.

The author's daughter, Jane

There were trips to Scotland to see Mona's family in Dumfriesshire. I was lucky to have an annual invitation from David de Stacpoole to fish the Spey at Craigellachie. David had worked with me in Cyprus in 1981. He was a pretty average tennis partner but could cast a superb longline on the river!

Notwithstanding an active retirement, which included trips to Dulwich to see elder daughter, Jackie and her two boys, I yearned to get back to France. Mona was slowly melting to the idea of a final adventure. Perhaps to live in France for five years? We contacted my sister, Caroline, and her husband Tim, Porter; he was the former ADC to General McMeekin at Bulford who I had worked for. They lived in a beautiful, restored house at Auvillar on the bank of the River Garonne. They moved to Auvillar from Paris. Tim was retiring and had just completed his last job as an attaché at the Embassy in Paris.

We had many a good holiday in the area. They were generous hosts and we fell in love with that bit of France. Carrie came up trumps having met someone in Marsac, twenty minutes away, whose house was for sale. Subsequently we all went to see La Maison Au Village, Marsac.

It was 'une maison bourgeoise' with three storeys, a large salon below, a big kitchen/dining hall on the ground floor, and heavily beamed bedroooms above. There was a controllable garden but no pool. The views over the countryside were outstanding.

A deal was done, and a pool installed. It just so happened that summer of 2003 when we moved was one of the hottest. The four of us had to assist the English removal people who were visibly wilting in 40° plus! The sight of our two daughters carrying sofas and armchairs down the narrow drive was forever inspiring.

Life in south west France had a pace all of its own – very gentle and there is always a tomorrow. I continued with another teacher, the French lessons that I had been having in England with the charming Odile. Mona also was doing some French with another tutor.

By the start of this last adventure, we were in our middle to late 70s. Inevitably we would need a doctor from time to time; Dr Smaile was based on Lavit, only a couple of kilometres up the road. Referral by the Doctor was to La Clinique in Montauban which provided a magnificent service. We both found the French health system excellent. Everyone had to have insurance which contributed towards serious illness. Additionally, all had to pay the Doctor's surgery 20 euros for each visit. A system that prevented unnecessary visits.

I have to say that we both benefitted hugely from treatment at La Clinique in Montauban. I had a double hernia fixed there, and Mona had the good fortune to survive some remarkable surgery. Unbeknown to us, she had fractured her neck subsequent to a fall.

Straight to Montauban in an ambulance accompanied by Les Pompiers. Seen by a young French surgeon, who successfully performed a delicate operation. Mona was in a private room for nearly three weeks at the Clinic. On picking her up with the car, I settled the bill for her treatment and, quite remarkably, the cost was less than to service our car … Vivre les services de santé!

Food in the south west was mainly based on local produce of goose and duck eg, Pate de Foie Gras and Confit de Canard. Delicious as they are, one can tire of them! The weekly, sometimes twice-weekly markets are superb. I don't know what it is – 'je ne sais quoi' – but there is something in the air that is attributable only to France; long may it last!

During our time in France, we had many visitors from family and friends. Hugo and Oliver, Jackie's boys, never left the pool; certainly not to walk to the baker in the village and ask for a baguette in French! The boys, I think, really enjoyed their trips to France – a spot of freedom, and not least a touch of colour. Glorious sunflowers at one side of the house and Oliver was fascinated with them, took some seeds, dried them and grew them in the garden at Dulwich! They organised fireworks, and barbecues, and played a lot of badminton on the lawn. They also both much enjoyed French

La Maison Au Village, Marsac

food and I recall Oliver, about six years old, trying his first half dozen oysters in a local restaurant. Hugo, meanwhile, has become an excellent, although expensive, cook! We had some amazing days out in the countryside, not least watching the French hunt wild boar with dogs.

We sometimes encouraged visitors to go to Collioure, on the Mediterranean coast adjacent to the Spanish border. The area is well known for its good anchovy harvests. Because of the exceptional light conditions in the area of Collioure, it became a magnet for many artists, such as Degas, Matisse, and Picasso, who lived nearby. Jane and daughter Jessica had a great time in Collioure in the middle of a visit to us. Mona and I also found a delightful boutique hotel just across the border into Spain.

From south west France one could be on the Mediterranean coast in five hours by car, the Atlantic coast, and the Basque country within three hours. Skiing in the Pyrenees was also an option but sadly we had outgrown that.

Another fairly local attraction was the Toulouse Lautrec museum at Albi. Packed with his drawings, paintings, and water colours. A few yards away is the Cathedral Basilica of Saint Cecilia. A magnificent edifice reaching up 79 metres. A visit to Albi, normally expected by guests, was a 4-hour return trip. I suppose that was part of the service!

We had planned five years in France and now we were in our sixth year. Time to go back home I suggested but Mona, who had come with reservations, did not want to leave! We returned to Wiltshire in late 2010. Au revoir to a soldier's life, adieu, La Belle France!

23

Back in England

"You both loved France, so why did you return to Wiltshire?" – I hear you say. The answer is quite simple, I did not wish to be buried in France; a foreign land with which neither Mona nor I had any roots. We settled for Wiltshire where we had spent our many years in military housing, or houses of our choice. I got to know the area of South West Wiltshire well when I attended a course early in 1953 at the School of Infantry, Warminster.

Before leaving for France in 2003, we lived in Fonthill Gifford; a delightful spot surrounded by woodland. Our three young grandchildren, learned about the abundance of wildflowers, the wild garlic, the deer, and not least, they learned about leadership; we would try and 'lose' them in the woods and then wait to see who took the lead to get us all home! A favourite game with the grandchildren was to enter this wild wood and imagine it was full, not only of deer, but tigers and wolves and Indian chiefs with bows and arrows. We strode along, "Hugo, look – a Tiger". Hugo, aged six, visibly blanched, "Oh my God" he said. I snapped a stick behind my back, "an arrow", I said. "RUN" cried all three. What fun we had!!

Sadly, another mistake in my life. We sold Vine Cottage in order that we could buy the property in France. Thus, on return to England in 2010, we were homeless! It was not actually quite so stark. Before leaving France, I had been in touch with the Fonthill Estate to enquire if they had any property available for short term rent and in due

Vine Cottage, Fonthill Gifford

course, we were offered the refurbished Fishing Lodge overlooking Fonthill lake.

The lodge was simply delightful. I think we might have been the first tenants as everything was in pristine order. Many happy walks around the lake passing the casting platform where with local guidance one could improve casting skills for trout or salmon – not fishing!

It was not long before I was in touch with local estate agents to try and find a small property suited to the two of us. This was easier said than done. The property market was in drought in early 2011. One or two properties did come up and were either too large or unsuitable for us. Eventually, whilst we were still in the Fishing Lodge, a tiny cottage became available in Hindon. Perfect for us. Two bathrooms, a tiny walled garden without a lawn! Hindon has proved to be a very friendly village with much going on between the Village Hall, the Church, the Fellowship Club, and the Surgery, and, not least, the village shop. The latter is run completely by village volunteers including a manager and post office enabler. From wine provided by a London vintner to meat provided by a local butcher; and offering hand delivered groceries to the doors of the less able bodied. We are very lucky and the envy of many.

The countryside nearby is quite stunning, with broad landscapes offering views without a house in sight, amazing walks, fishing on the Wylye and Nadder rivers, and some shoots which are regularly supported by Beaters from the village. I am very confident that we made the right decision to return from our French idyll. There can be few places as beautiful, relaxing, and friendly as this small piece of Wiltshire.

Hatch House, River Wyle

Epilogue

On the plus-side: excitement, comradeship, travel, and trouble-shooting are the Author's abiding memories of his fulfilling time in the Army. On the negative side is a sense of less than proper reward for service given and endured by all ranks.

Proper reward encompasses nothing more than the best possible pay and conditions of service to match the military 'Can Do' approach to duty, met, it has to be said, without any proper regard to family circumstances.

The level of operational activity taken on by the Army since Korea is remarkable. To name a few:-

- MALAYA
- KUWAIT
- KENYA
- FALKLANDS
- IRAQ
- AFGHANISTAN
- CANAL ZONE, EGYPT
- SIERRA LEONE
- CYPRUS
- BORNEO
- SUEZ
- BOSNIA
- NORTHERN IRELAND

At the time of such conflicts, the Army was roughly at a strength of 150,000 plus. It is now to be reduced to 72,000. Robotics, drones and rockets are to be the conflict winners? Such wisdom is questioned.

Terrorism and factionalism have inexorably increased worldwide. Notwithstanding overt actions, there lurks covert activity in the shape of Artificial Intelligence (AI), and Cyber Warfare. In the wings, China is asserting itself, both militarily and economically. Hostilities in the Arctic, or in Space, cannot be too distant.

It remains vital to keep ahead in all fields of technology, not least the military applications. However, the experiences bequeathed by the conflicts listed above involving UK armed forces demonstrate the enduring need for 'boots on the ground'. A gentle reminder: only boots on the ground could have won the day against communist terrorists in the 12-year Malaya Emergency. Likewise, in Kenya and Borneo. What of Africa; the spread of jihadism, coupled with Chinese expansion?

The first duty of the Government is the protection of the United Kingdom. This cannot be done by regular forces subject to withering manpower levels whilst trying to fulfil responsibilities around the world. Reward, legalise and train the Territorial Army properly to provide timely support in aid of the Police and Civil Authorities.

The reader may detect that little has changed in the challenge of military duty between now and the time the Author served. That is in the context of the pressures on a volunteer 'Can Do' army reacting to constant deployments and sacrificial family life coupled with degrading pay and conditions of service.

Much needs to be done to recruit and retain personnel in the armed services for the future.

The Government will get the Army it is prepared to pay for. To keep up with technology is paramount but never forget it is soldiers in the field that win the day.

Acknowledgements

The memoir is entirely my own work and based on a memory of fact not fiction. I have used names of persons and places which, to the best of my knowledge are accurate. I seek forgiveness for any inaccuracies or hurt to any person.

I am indebted to family and some friends who over the years have encouraged me to write a memoir. In terms of the printed words, I am especially grateful to Victoria Louth, a freelance Personal Assistant, who had the task of transcribing my appalling handwriting onto a computer. I am grateful too, to village neighbours who have spurred me on.

I owe a special debt to Renée Knight, the Author, who has seen early drafts and offered me much valuable comment and advice.

PMD
Hindon 2021

About the Author

The Author was educated at Charterhouse. He started his National Service in January 1950 as a private soldier in The Sherwood Foresters. He completed his service to the nation in 1986 as a two-star general.

He has travelled and lived all over the world, including Korea, Malaysia, Egypt, Cyrpus, Libya, and Berlin.

He is a graduate of the Staff College, The National Defence College, and The Royal College of Defence Studies.

The Author was married to Mona (neé Wallace) for 63 years. Tragically both Mona and much-loved elder daughter Jacqueline passed away in 2020. This book is in their memory.

BV - #0043 - 091221 - C14 - 210/148/9 [11] - CB - 9781913012571 - Gloss Lamination